ⁱoᵢ

ɋuested by other

on, in

the

GATELY

The Life and ⁱⁱⁱⁱ ⁱ *a Pop Icon*

GATELY

The Life and Death of a Pop Icon

Paul Martin

KNA Media Ltd.

First published in 2010 by

KNA Media Ltd.
Woodbrook
Termon Feckin
County Louth
Ireland

ISBN: 978-0-956663-0-7

10 9 8 7 6 5 4 3 2 1

PRINt
IRISH
CLÓBHUAILÍ
IN éIRINN

Front cover image © Irish Daily Mirror
Back cover image © Collins Picture Agency Dublin
Designed, typeset, printed and bound in Ireland by Anglo Printers

I would like to dedicate this book to the memory of Stephen Gately, to my wife Sinead who kept me sane with endless cups of tea as I wrote, and to my beautiful children.

ACKNOWLEDGEMENTS

Firstly I wish to thank my wife Sinead for supporting and keeping me motivated throughout the process of writing this book – even through her morning sickness. I couldn't have done it without you.

A special thanks to my editor John Kierans, who sent me around the world in hot pursuit of Boyzone stories over the years, and who drove this book from an idea and turned it into a reality.

The publication of this book could not have been possible but for the ungrudging efforts put in by a large number of individuals including my colleague Sarah Bardon, whose endless files of research were a Godsend. In addition I would also like to thank Zoe Watson for all her help with the pictures, Paul Feldstein from The Feldstein Agency and James O'Leary as well as all my colleagues in the Irish Mirror.

Finally I would like to thank Louis Walsh for taking my phone call and giving me my first big showbiz story 13 years ago – on Stephen Gately! Your patience, help and encouragement over the years will never be forgotten.

TABLE OF CONTENTS

CHAPTER ONE

Death of a Superstar

As their plane was about to touch down amidst the glistening Palma skyline, Stephen Gately must have felt that he and his husband Andrew really deserved a break, and that this holiday was going to be a trip to remember.

Descending foot by foot towards the jet black tarmac that would welcome them to their dream getaway, Stephen broke into a smile, remembering how they had promised themselves this break just four months earlier, when Boyzone kicked off their sell-out tour.

Stephen arrived in Majorca feeling a mixture of exhaustion and elation, having just completed a gruelling run of sell-out shows which attracted over 130,000 fans and cemented the band's comeback in spectacular style. Stephen had basked in the limelight on stage and savoured every second, revelling in the regained glory of life in a pop supergroup, enjoying the euphoria of stardom that might so easily have been lost forever.

Two years on from their celebrated reunion, Stephen and his Boyzone brothers were back on top of the world, conquering the charts and revelling in the glory of the big time all over again. As their plane taxied along the runway, passengers in the aisles behind them clattered around excitedly, grabbing bags and newspapers and powering up their phones.

Buoyant with anticipation of their month-long break, Stephen gathered up the scraps of paper he had scribbled on feverishly throughout the flight and placed them carefully in his black designer hold-all. To a bystander they would have appeared to be little more than tiny notes, scribbled hastily in black ink to while away the three-hour flight.

But to Stephen they were much more than that. They were the secrets that held the key to the dramatic climax of his first novel, which he was agonisingly close to completing.

This holiday would take care of that. "We're going to mix business with pleasure," Stephen told his family as they set off on the trip. "I'm finishing my book and then I'm going to celebrate."

For Stephen and Andy there was plenty to rejoice over. Stephen had just laid down the vocals for a new Boyzone single, Gave It All Away, which would signal their return to the pop charts with a sophisticated and exploratory new sound.

As their taxi weaved around the dusty roads of Port D'Antrax towards their villa, Stephen surveyed the breathtaking mountain terrain that led to their secret bolt-hole. He smiled to himself and looked across the car to Andrew – the man whom had helped him escape from a life of secrecy and heartache to find his true self. Andrew had dutifully attended almost every one of Stephen's concerts spanning the previous May and June. Now it was their time.

Their relationship, which had once been volatile, had now settled into a harmonious understanding and was going from strength to strength, propelled by the marriage vows they had taken three years before. While Andy knew that their relationship might take second place to Stephen's frantic touring and promotional commitments, now he could look forward to re-connecting and focusing on what they both held in the highest esteem - each other.

Their Majorca hideaway was the one place that was theirs and only theirs; somewhere that neither the press nor Stephen's fans had yet discovered. For the first time in months Stephen could truly let go of the pressures of fame and life in a boy band and concentrate on his love for Andrew. He must have felt truly content and relaxed for the first time in months, as the taxi took the final turn around the curving mountain road and pulled up to the shiny black gates of their holiday villa that harboured so many precious memories.

Andrew grabbed the bags while Stephen opened the mailbox, adorned with their names that he had proudly etched in black biro as soon as they sealed the deal and bought the property for €1.1 million.

They spent those first days of the trip proudly decorating their living room and bedrooms, making sure everything was perfect for the influx of friends and family who would fly out to join them over the course of their vacation. Andy would dash to the nearby harbour to buy ornate picture frames which would adorn photographs of him and Stephen taken on their travels around the world. Stephen picked colour schemes and filled every corner of the villa with fresh flowers from the local market, blossoming in an explosion of colour that seemed to match the exhilaration and optimism he felt. Life was good and the future was bright – and this trip would be the celebration of their past achievements and future ambitions.

For their friends in the tightly-knit community, Stephen and Andy's arrival was always welcome. In reality they were far from the party-mad showbiz couple people may have warily expected when they first moved in.

As their neighbour Graham McDowell explained: "Stephen was the most charming person you could wish to meet. He was totally genuine. I sat near him a couple of times on flights chatting to him. He was a very quiet person. On one flight I asked if he'd like a glass of wine, as I was getting one. His reaction was, 'Actually I'll just have an orange juice. I rarely drink.' There are quite a few famous people living in Andratx. They choose to live here because although it's a very luxurious area, people are left alone."

A waitress in their favourite local bar, Gran Folies, agreed: "Stephen and Andy were regulars here over the summer. They seemed like a very nice couple – very polite. We knew Stephen was a singer but he was very modest. They would often come here for a beer or two, but I wouldn't say they were heavy drinkers."

Stephen and Andy had fallen in love with the plush resort from the moment they first visited on holiday a year before. For those who have money to burn, Andratx was a seductively discreet and upmarket enclave where money talked and privacy could be virtually guaranteed. It was everything that a world famous pop star could dream of and Stephen, having made millions with his chart topping exploits, could take his pick of the finest villas.

With only 8,000 residents it was little wonder a host of other stars invested in sprawling holiday homes, which would act as the perfect summer refuge from the trials and tribulations of life in the spotlight. Supermodel Claudia Schiffer and movie star Tom Cruise joined multi-millionaire sports idols like Michael Schumacher to lap up the balmy temperatures, enjoy the fine seafood and splash out in the ultra exclusive designer stores. The town also had a reputation for attracting celebrities of a bygone era, including the Natacha Rambova, second wife of a male icon from an earlier era, Rudolph Valentino, who lived in the area during the 1930's.

It was the rustic charm coupled with the cosmopolitan ambience and allure of the sun-drenched coastal resort that offered so much to Stephen and Andy. Stephen would while away the lazy afternoons strolling around the Marina and sipping coffees in the waterside cafes as he flicked through the English newspapers, before returning to their villa for long evenings sipping wine on the balcony as the sun set over the picturesque groves and rolling terrain of the island's scenic east coast.

Inside their apartment no expense was spared: luxurious trappings and the best of everything. Shiny door-to-door marble floors glistened as a searing sun streamed through the openings in the dark wooden shutters. Each of the five rooms was adorned with the most expensive fabrics and furniture, along with the best home entertainment systems. For anyone lucky enough to set foot in their villa it was an experience never to be forgotten.

Outside, the couple had created a small oasis of climbing plants and blossoming flowers, where they would sit enjoying alfresco breakfasts at their leisure before strolling to the local markets to stock up on fresh produce. Everywhere, the heady scent of jasmine and bougainvillea filled the air and heightened the senses, all the more potent as night fell and the chirping of crickets reached a crescendo.

"There was always equipment being brought in and out of the house," said a neighbour. "One day it would be a new table and chairs, the next it would be a big screen plasma TV from a local store. They didn't waste any time creating a real home away from home. It was clear from all the money they were spending on the villa that they saw it as more than just a two weeks-a-year holiday home. They always openly said to the others in the area that they wanted to live here for six months-a-year. But they were both very busy with their workloads back in the UK so it never really seemed to work out like that.

"But they were definitely part of the furniture in the Andratx community and there wasn't one person who would have said a bad word about them. They had the money but they weren't all flashy. They were happy just doing the normal things everyone else in the area did."

As Andrew prepared lunch, Stephen's mobile phone ringer reverberated from the rocky landscape around them with a message from one of his bandmates. Basking in the sunshine and wearing his favourite pair of designer sunglasses, Stephen opened his in-box to see a text from Ronan Keating: *"I've just heard your vocals on that track. They are out of this world. This song is going to be big,"* he enthused. Stephen broke into a coy smile.

His mind wandered back to just three months earlier where he had stood, teary eyed, on the stage of London's o2 arena on the final night of their sell out tour. He could still feel the convulsions through his body from that feeling of adulation as 13,000 fans chanted his name in unison. Their next year, he told to himself, would be even bigger. Still smiling, he texted his reply: *"Love the new songs, pal. Can't wait for the new record. Love you, straw balls. Speak later."*

But Stephen was far from content to bask in the glory of Boyzone's impressive comeback. He had vowed at the end of their last tour that they would "take it to the next level" at the end of the year and release their greatest album ever. He was driven by a desire to outshine anything they had done previously in their career, and with a sell-out tour behind them, plans were already afoot for the next big project.

Central to these big ambitions was Louis Walsh who, over the previous two years, had grown particularly close to Stephen as they began working together again following Boyzone's comeback. Louis would readily tell his friends in the media that Stephen was his favourite member of the group: "He's just so down to earth, nothing has changed him. All the success, money, everything. He's just a good human being. The thing about Stephen is he's not one of these manipulative self-centred singers who think they have a divine right to be rich and famous. He is as humble a person as you will ever meet. That's why I want to keep working with him. He's so refreshing."

With these big plans in mind, Louis had been locked in an intense conversation with Stephen just a week before he flew to Majorca, when they had partied the night away together at the Mirror Pride of Britain Awards.

"He was so enthusiastic about the future that night," Louis reflected. "He told me he was going off on holiday then coming back with all guns blazing. What people didn't realise about Stephen was that he was totally driven and so ambitious. His energy was on a different level to anyone else's. So when he went off on that trip to Majorca it was to take a break and then come back and launch into some incredible projects. He was really excited about his book too.

"He would have gone back into the studios and started recording the new album, and he was already coming up with big ideas for the next tour. Stephen never really switched off totally. It was always about the next big thing for him and that's what made him so successful."

True to Louis' word, even as he lapped up the blissful Majorca sunshine, Stephen didn't lose sight of the fact that he needed to take care of unfinished business. He had promised himself that he would finally complete work on the fantasy novel he had spent years creating and reworking to fulfil a life-long dream of becoming a published author.

Just weeks earlier, that dream seemed to be moving towards reality when he landed a publishing deal with the major London-based publisher Hodder & Stoughton, who planned to release the novel by Christmas – providing Stephen could meet his deadline and deliver by the end of October. The publishers were so confident that his novel would be a success that they forwarded him a £50,000 advance and promised him the backing of a huge distribution deal and marketing campaign.

"The story had been in his head for years," Andy would later recall. "He was always talking about it, so one day I registered the domain name."

Andrew's motives were twofold. He remembers Stephen was going through a frustrated phase. "He had too much time on his hands – and sometimes I think he forgot that I was running a business. Even though we had a housekeeper, he had got into doing housework – he could be very fastidious – and then he was unhappy because he was at home every day cleaning. That was when I said that perhaps he should get started on the book.

"The book was escapism, but it was also his way of battling with his demons. As he was writing it, you could see him shedding his worries and growing more confident."

Writing his novel was never a chore – more a labour of love. As a child and teenager growing up in the north side of Dublin he had often felt sidelined as he struggled to fit in with his peers, preferring to lose himself in the fantasy worlds on the pages of well-thumbed Terry Pratchett and CS Lewis fantasy novels, which offered the ultimate escapism for a boy with no direction.

Now he could finally create his own world of fantasy and magic for children to enjoy. And even on holiday, there wasn't a minute to be wasted. Stephen grabbed his red laptop and moved into the bedroom where Andrew had already taken up a seat at the mahogany desk to check his work emails and begin work on a computer programme that was nearing deadline.

Stephen fluffed up the pillows on the bed and powered up his computer, clicking on the icon that read simply *The Tree of Seasons*. He scrolled down the hundreds of pages of meticulously written passages that had sprung from four years of tireless work. He had poured every emotion into those words and now he was reaching the end – the final chapter. He grabbed the notes scribbled on the flight and began to apply the finishing touches.

Every now and again Stephen would excitedly shout out to Andrew as he banged the keys at lightning speed "I've got a great idea for the finish," before explaining how each character would figure in his dramatic climax. Andrew, still with his back to him, would reply intermittently "Yes baby, that's great. I'm trying to concentrate."

Before long Stephen beckoned Andrew across the room for a hug. "I'm so excited about this," he said. "Let's go out tonight and celebrate. This has been four years in the making."

***

That night they dressed up and headed out for dinner at 9 p.m. They ate in their favourite harbour-side restaurant and talked about their plans for the coming weeks, ordering a second bottle of white wine as they soaked up the last of the evening sunshine and they began to make plans for the rest of the evening.

First they went to Aries nightclub where Stephen, in keeping with the party spirit, ordered a small bottle of cava. But after precisely 36 minutes Stephen settled their bill and the pair walked 50 yards down the road to the Euphoria bar, where among the revellers was 25-year-old Bulgarian waiter, Georgi Dochev.

He was slim and handsome, well known to locals and an active member of the town's gay community. By now Stephen was loosening up and in high spirits. Spurred on by the wine and the party music, he and Andrew resigned themselves to a night on the tiles, ordering more champagne and wine and inviting Georgi to join them at their table.

After finishing their drinks they jumped into a taxi and moved on to the city's most famous late-night gay club, the Black Cat. With its dungeon chambers, grimy walls and transvestite theme nights, it was a million miles from the kind of up-market showbiz haunts they frequented at home. As one regular clubber put it: "This wouldn't be the kind of place you'd come to for a nice civilised night. It has a bit of a reputation. Stephen and Andy had been there before a few times and they liked that they didn't attract too much attention there, unlike when they went clubbing in London."

Stephen would never have dreamed of being spotted at a place like this when he was on the radar in the UK or Ireland. The club's reputation would not have sat comfortably with his image as the clean-cut cutesy pop pin-up he projected to his loyal fans. But here, Stephen was just another face in the crowd and he could let his hair down and indulge in the carefree atmosphere of the city's most hedonistic night spot without the worry of paparazzi snapping him or a clubber selling the story. Tonight he could be himself.

As they walked up towards the doormen Stephen was in triumphant form. He burst into an impromptu version of Michael Jackson's *The Way You Make Me Feel*, inviting Andy and Georgi to join him. It was clear the party was well and truly underway and Stephen, as in his exhilarating stage shows with Boyzone, was happy to be the centre of attention. "He looked so happy and carefree," Georgi would later remark in his only newspaper interview. "He didn't seem to have a care in the world."

Georgi was equally happy to enjoy the carefree indulgences of a night with a pop star. Knowing Stephen and Andrew would stump up for the drinks bill wasn't to be scoffed at when you were a ten euro-an-hour waiter. They ordered more champagne and wine and flirted openly with each other in front of the oblivious clubbers on the dance floor.

As revellers danced amid the haze of swirling lights and deafening dance music, Stephen and Andrew grew increasingly tipsy, loosening up with every glass of the €60-a-bottle bubbly that was now flowing. At this point Stephen struck up a conversation with a clubber who was invited back to their table. After drinking together one of the group handed Stephen a small bag of marijuana. He slipped it into his jeans pocket and reached over to hug Andrew again, as if to say that, even amid this sexually charged atmosphere, he was still very much on his mind.

By now it was around 4 a.m. and Stephen, sitting between Georgi and Andrew, was clearly feeling the effects of a night on the booze. He polished off the last of his champagne and then turned to Georgi. "Would you like to come back to our place for a few drinks?" he asked. "We're getting a taxi back now. You're more than welcome."

Georgi didn't have to think twice. His world of waiting tables and scraping a living together was a million miles from the lavish lifestyle that his suitors for the evening enjoyed. He nodded and smiled, and then the trio climbed wearily to their feet and bid their farewells to other clubbers who had congregated around their table. As they took the 45 minute taxi ride home, Stephen and Andy sat in the back, cracking jokes and making small talk with their guest, whose broken English was enough to get him through a disjointed conversation with the couple.

Just hours earlier, Stephen and Andrew had been lovingly sharing their dreams and hopes for the future as they sat in the afternoon sunshine at their villa. The contrast as they swept back up to the gates in the taxi could not have been starker. Now the night's encounter took a darker turn that, for some, would taint the image of a devoted couple.

As they arrived at the villa Stephen did something that would have shocked his loyal fans to the core. He strolled languidly to the living room, sat down, took a small bag of marijuana from his pocket and slowly rolled a joint. After lighting it he took a brief drag before joining Andrew and Georgi on the sofa.

Stephen had always claimed that Boyzone were a strictly anti-drugs band and had never felt the need to indulge because they preferred to do things the Irish way and drink their rival bands under the table. But his actions in the villa that evening told a different story about him.

All three were now extremely drunk. Georgi would later explain: "I think he made the joint with pure marijuana – I didn't see him mix in any tobacco, and it had a really strong smell."

Since marrying Andrew in 2006 the pair had gone to great lengths to portray a picture perfect relationship. Stephen always knew that any report of hedonistic behaviour could spell disaster for his pop career and tarnish that romance. But news reports and speculation about what happened in the hours after they returned from the nightclub ultimately did cast a shadow over the image of a dedicated, loving couple.

That morning in their villa such concerns had seemed a million miles away.

According to Georgi, Stephen grew tired from his night of boozing and smoking and called it to a halt. Wearing just underwear and a black tee-shirt, he gently kissed Andy goodnight, lay on the sofa and drifted off to sleep. "He went to the bathroom," said Georgi. "He came back but very quickly dozed off. He was lying with his head on my chest, snoring. At around 5.30 a.m. Andy fell asleep beside him, so I went into one of the bedrooms and went to sleep."

Two-and-a-half hours later, at around 8 a.m., Georgi bolted up in the bed, awoken by the abrupt chime of the doorbell. Confused and disorientated, he walked wearily back to the living room to alert Andy to the commotion at the door. But he found him lying with Stephen, his arm gently tucked under Stephen's torso and they looked at peace. "It's not my house, I can't answer the door," he reasoned with himself and he returned back to the bedroom. Moments later Andy himself woke up and sluggishly shuffled to his own bedroom, leaving Stephen in what he thought was a deep sleep on the sofa.

At 10.30 a.m. Georgi woke again and this time sat down on the chair next to where Stephen was still lying. He lit a cigarette and sipped a glass of water as he surveyed the stale scene of stubbed out butts in the ashtray and empty glasses through bleary eyes. "I noticed he was in exactly the same position, sort of curled up with his face obscured by a cushion," Georgi recalled of that fateful morning. "But I didn't want to disturb him and went back to bed."

At 1 p.m. Georgi, still unable to fall into a deep sleep, quietly climbed out of bed. He spent fifteen minutes showering in the pristine bathroom the couple had decorated on their last visit to the villa earlier in the summer. Andy remained asleep. Georgi checked his text messages and then dressed before sitting down on the sofa next to Stephen. It was only then that he realised something wasn't right. Stephen was lying on the sofa in the exact same position he had been in hours earlier – with his face still semi-buried in a cushion.

He moved close to him, gently touching his head. No response. Then, with more force, he shook his arm to try and trigger a reaction. Still no response. The first signs of panic set in. Then he noticed that Stephen was cold and white, and his body limp. His heart began pounding, his head swirling in a frenzy of fear and anxiety. Almost tripping in blind panic as he leapt up, Georgi burst through the door of Andy's bedroom. "Come quickly," he screamed in his broken English. "It's Stephen. Is he all right?"

Andy threw back his white linen covers and bolted towards the doorway, rushing in to find Stephen still sprawled across the sofa in the same position. He stood over him momentarily, then knelt down beside his lifeless body. "Baby.....baby?" he whispered in his ear, praying for a reaction. But there was nothing. In desperation Andy beckoned to Georgi. "Help me get him up. Quickly for God's sake," he shouted, his voice becoming more and more urgent.

As they lifted Stephen from the sofa, blind panic took over. "Andy then picked him up and we noticed there was a yellowish liquid around his mouth and on the sofa where he had been lying," Georgi explained. "But it was impossible to give him first aid. His body was stiff and his jaw was rigid."

In a last desperate bid to save Stephen, Andy screamed: "Call for an ambulance quickly. Please God." Andy, now in floods of tears continued to plead in vain for Stephen to wake. "Come on baby, wake up, baby please wake up," he urged, rocking him in his arms, his face a picture of utter despair.

By the time the ambulance pulled up through the electronic gates, a crowd of neighbours had gathered outside in the searing heat. The medics brushed past the onlookers who had gathered on the steps of the apartment and were frantically speculating over what was going on.

The doctor rushed to Stephen's body and gently prized him from a distraught Andy's arms. He cleared Stephen's airways and checked the singer's pulse, but it was clear nothing could be done. Taking a deep breath and turning to Andy, who was now lying on the floor sobbing against the sofa, he gently announced: "I'm sorry to say this, but there is nothing I can do. Stephen is dead."

CHAPTER TWO

From Rags to Riches

Stephen gripped the pencil tightly between his thumb and forefinger, biting his lip in firm concentration. Once again, he scrolled his name in dramatic handwriting, emphasising the grand letters a little more this time, before pulling his head back and proudly surveying his work.

"What the fuck are you at?" came a voice from behind. The budding star spun round, snapping out of his self-indulgent daydream. Before he could answer his classmate had grabbed the copy book and was flicking through page upon page of the pompous scrawl. He glared at it in disbelief. Stephen Gately. Signed dozens of times, each attempt with more flair and pizzazz than the last. Stars had been doodled on the edges of the page.

"I'm practicing for when I'm famous," Stephen shrugged impassively.

The boy laughed before looking in the young schoolboy's eyes and realising that this young fool was deadly serious. He clipped the back of his tousled head with the notebook before throwing away the book in disgust. "Get a grip, who do you think you are?" he snorted as he stormed out of the classroom.

Undeterred, Stephen ripped out the top page and threw it after him. "Keep it for when I'm famous," he shouted, "it'll be worth a lot of money some day." He could feel his cheeks burn as he yelled out defiantly. But it was too late – the boy had disappeared into the hallway.

It was 1990 and the young Gately was attending Strand Technical College in inner-city Dublin. At 14 the young dreamer was used to the jibes. Having spent his early years growing up on Upper Oriel Street, just off Sherriff Street in Dublin's tough inner-city, he had learned very quickly that being different wasn't an easy badge to wear.

He had always wanted to be rich and famous. And this inner-city dreamer wasn't shy about shouting it from those dingy Dublin rooftops. Years later, after raking in millions from sell-out concerts and number one hits, he would recall how he used to fray his classmates' nerves.

"I went around everywhere signing autographs for people," he confessed. "My school pals got so fed up with it, but I used to tell them to hang on to the pieces of paper because they would be worth a fortune some day. My family were always supportive of me but they didn't know anything about the entertainment industry. And I didn't realise how much hard work it would be."

The closest his family ever got to a passion for music was when they got together after a couple of pints of stout. His father would sit back, commanding the room's attention as he belted out ballad after old Irish ballad, accompanied by his mother on the spoons.

But for Stephen – born in 1976 to Martin, a painter/decorator, and Margaret, a part-time cleaner – the glamour of the entertainment industry was still a distant dream. The second of five brothers and sisters, he knew all too well from an early age the tough side of life.

The majority of his clothes were hand-me-downs from his older siblings and for a time he shared a bed with his sister. Indeed, he saw too many days when he was reminded that his tight-knit family were not as well off as others in the working class community.

"Mam," a young Stephen bounded into the kitchen after school one sunny afternoon. "All the kids are going on a trip away. The teachers are organising it." The words spilled out as he tried to catch his breath from the five-minute sprint home from school. The exertions of running meant that the cardboard used to cover the holes in his shoes was now protruding from the gaps, and Gately sat on the kitchen chair plugging the brown paper back into place.

"You won't believe where we're going," he told her, his excitement steaming full-speed ahead.

But his mother wasn't long in putting an end to his innocent enthusiasm. With seven mouths to feed, childhood holidays were a treat they could rarely afford. Tears welled up in the boy's eyes as he tried to protest. "I'll look stupid. All the other kids are going. It's not fair," he cried, storming off to wallow in his misfortune.

A short while later he returned to find his mother sitting in silence, alone and emotional. Tears streamed down her face at her disappointment and sadness that she couldn't give her young son the simple childhood treats he deserved.

Stephen Gately would carry that stark memory with him as a man, many years later, as he travelled the world in private jets and lived it up in five star luxury hotels. His mother had done her very best – he just couldn't see it at the time.

For his part, his father Martin also taught his son the essence of hard work. On days off school he used to bring a young Stephen along to help him with his painting and decorating jobs, which Stephen, filled with dreams of a bigger and brighter future, loathed.

"Start on that wall over there and I'll see you right at the end of the day," Martin told the wannabee pop star as he handed him a paint-splattered scraper.

Dressed in old dungarees, the kind he wouldn't see again until his future bandmate Shane was prancing around the RTE studio during Boyzone's first infamous appearance on The Late Late Show, his son got to work. After scraping bare almost two dozen walls, back aching, hands raw and blistered, he'd open his palm for his reward. A pound was all his father could afford.

It was no wonder he wanted to escape from the poverty-stricken life he witnessed his family burden. In later years it was often reported how proud Stephen was of his roots. But in truth he was also haunted by a constant fear of not being able to break free from his impoverished beginnings. He saw what life was like without money, he witnessed the sacrifices his family had to make and - as he put it so bluntly in the Boyzone years "I didn't want to end up poor like my parents."

For Stephen, his dreams were far bigger than the suffocating surroundings of inner-city Dublin. His future lay beyond the stifling north and east walls that surrounded the high rise flats.

While the other kids hung out on street corners playing games such as knick knack and kiss catch, the budding singer was far more introverted and would escape into daydreams for hours on end. It was a way to cope with the dreary surroundings and allow his imagination to wander towards greater things and the stardom and acclaim he knew would one day be his.

Stephen was a soft-hearted, sensitive child. He loved nature. His mother would sometimes find the pint-sized child wrapped in a duvet, gazing out his window for hours as he watched the rain or, in the winter, a beautiful snowfall. In fact, in the latter years of his life, although surrounded by the distracting trappings of fame and fortune, he would still take refuge under a blanket for hours on end and watch the changing seasons unfold.

But as a child, when he didn't have the money some of the other children had to escape from the street on a holiday or an adventure, he made the most of his surroundings and as he recalled many years later: "It would cost nothing to walk around a park or to read a book."

Even the paranormal used to occupy the active youngster's imagination. One night, at the tender age of four, as he lay in bed waiting for sleep to come, he was convinced he saw the ghost of an old man walking around his room. He watched the figure in dead silence, unable to breathe and frozen in his spot, as it disappeared into thin air. Screaming the roof down and startling his family awake, his parents bounded into the room. Through tears and hysteria he tried to explain what had happened. His parents brushed it off as a silly nightmare and stayed with Stephen, stroking his forehead as he fell back to sleep.

But the next night Stephen's shrill scream could be heard throughout the tiny flat once more and the young child swore to his parents that his imagination wasn't running wild. He could see the ghost-like figure with his own two eyes. The vision soon became a regular occurrence.

Years later, at the height of his Boyzone career, Stephen still claimed his childhood apparitions were genuine. "When I was a kid there was this ghost of a man who used to come out. I used to see him all the time, and I'd scream. I was around four when I saw him for the first time; he was just walking around the flat, and he used to come out every night."

On the odd days that he did join in with the other kids he would spend his time in the playgrounds near his parents' flat. Swings, slides and a football pitch helped the children occupy their minds and once a year the tight-knit neighbourhood would have a community week where they would hold competitions for snooker, darts and fancy dress. At the end, all the kids would queue up and the organisers would hand out packets of crisps, sweets and a fizzy drink to each of them.

When they weren't playing the children were living off their wits. As a young boy, Stephen was still intent on making himself a few bob and would spend his time chopping up pallets to sell as kindling, or bagging potatoes all day for a bar of chocolate or a can of coke.

All the while, a part of Stephen that would play a significant role in his later years was beginning to emerge. As he reached puberty, unusual thoughts began to cross his mind, thoughts which he never entertained before. Soon the first inklings of his complex sexuality began to flicker.

One day his entire family were piled into the sitting room watching family television, and his brothers and sisters were bossing him around. "Get up and change the channel," they nudged, after he made their umpteenth cup of tea. He was a soft kid who didn't mind running around after his older family members or being told what to do.

He had just settled back into his chair when a handsome young man appeared on the screen. Stephen stared at him in silence, frozen to his seat, taking in his toned appearance. It stirred something inside that he had felt only a few times before. He was secretly turned on and blushed at the thought that his siblings might sense his growing excitement. He looked around but their attention was fixed to the screen. Did they know? He wondered. Certainly children had teased him about this kind of thing before.

At the time he had just left St. Laurence O'Toole Primary school, where he had become a regular victim of bullying. And at home, a small handful of children on the street didn't make life any easier.

"Faggot," they shouted, as he tried his best to put on a brave face and ignore their taunts. "The queer is going to cry. Look at him lads," one youngster laughed, "run home to your ma, ya pansy. Ask her why ya like cock."

Stephen felt the nausea rise. He hated their taunts. He dreaded the sinister moments when it would all start up again. He could be having fun on the street with the other kids, belly laughing at their innocent shenanigans and then all of a sudden one nasty youngster would decide to darken the mood. They would start off with a sneering comment. He'd try his best to block it out and carry on with his pastime. But, not getting the reaction they desired, they would soon start up again. Louder this time. Repeating the hurtful digs, until they pierced him to the core.

"Oi! I said 'Queer boy', are you listening to me?" bellowed the same child, more aggressively this time. Once again, it had become too much to take. Stephen suddenly abandoned the game and turned his back to walk home as his friends faded into the background, afraid to speak up and defend their pal, for fear they'd be next.

More often than not Stephen would hear the footsteps behind him, gathering pace, as he made his way home. The ring leader would decide to take off after him and on the unlucky days he was caught.

"When I'm calling you, you answer me you fucking twerp. D'ya hear me? You're a fucking queer," bellowed the bully into his face. Pinned to the ground, he squeezed his eyes shut, praying for his beating to be over. A couple of hard digs and Stephen would be sent on his way, bruised and battered and with a heavy heart.

Once in the door, his mother would be waiting, clutching her chest with that same worried look on her face. She was all too familiar with the taunts. "Are you all right pet?" she quizzed. "Yeah I'm fine ma, it's grand." "What were they saying to you love," she asked again. "Nothing ma, it's cool, just leave it, ok?"

Later Margaret would recall how Stephen never wanted to talk about the cruelty he suffered at the hands of a few nasty children. He would keep to himself; mull it over in his head, afraid of what people might think if he let his real feelings be known. It was a fear that would haunt him well into the days of his boy band success.

But for now, this boy from Sherriff Street saw his sexuality as something he must hide at all costs. He could never imagine that one day this same "dark secret" would make him front page news in *The New York Times*.

***

There was one boy who was not like the others. Young Stephen Gately had developed a strong bond with him from an early age and was now beginning to feel the first flutters of teenage romance. His name was Steve Howard.

The two Dubliners were life-long friends for as long as they could remember. The boys had known each other since they were kids playing in the tough inner city streets around Sheriff Street and with time they became inseparable. They did everything together, entering dance and talent competitions, and were often seen in their own little world, laughing and joking at each other's private quips. They would play conkers together, carve weapons out of wood and play fight. Where one went, the other followed and nothing could tear them apart.

In his budding music career, Steve Howard was a good friend

to Stephen, encouraging him to enter all the local dance gigs. He knew his friend was destined for show business and the two shared a deep-rooted passion for the stage. He was there to witness Stephen star in the lead role in his junior school production of *Joseph and the Amazing Technicolor Dreamcoat*. And when he was older, Steve Howard joined the Gaiety Theatre group in Dublin city centre. All the while, they were bonded by their love of performing arts and would spend many evenings choreographing new dance routines.

Howard was also friends with Stephen when he joined a disco dance troupe called Black Magic. The future boy band member was one of four boys in the troupe of 12, and Black Magic soon became a serious affair, with Steve Howard entering the group into competitions all over Dublin, leading them to win the all-Ireland Disco Dance finals when Stephen was just 13. And a year after that he encouraged Stephen to go for a job with the International Modelling agency in Dublin, where he modelled teenage clothes for some of Dublin's leading department stores.

It was Howard who was Stephen's constant companion when no one else would indulge him in his flights of fancy about stardom and sell-out tours. He was thrilled for the promising star when he landed his first TV appearance for Jo Maxi, after Stephen had directed a play called *Whether You Like it or Not*. And again he was proud of Stephen when his first taste of stardom came at 16, when Alan Parker filmed *The Commitments* around Dublin's Northside – giving many locals the chance to become film extras for the day.

As the two boys sat and watched Stephen on the big screen, Howard slapped him on the back and embraced him with pride. The pair laughed and joked about the start of big things to come, blissfully unaware of the separate tragedies that would eventually befall them.

As they grew older the boyhood pals began to realise they were gay and their relationship developed into something stronger. They started off privately experimenting with each other when they found themselves alone and away from prying eyes. On the first instance, Howard took the lead, lightly leaning forward to kiss Stephen on the lips. He pulled back to study his friend's reaction. For a moment Stephen looked stunned then gave him a little smile and leaning over, kissed him back. The excitement they felt gave them confidence that they were finally discovering their true sexuality, unbeknown to most of their friends, and certainly not their families – or so they thought.

When Stephen was fifteen years old he finally plucked up the courage to broach the subject with his sister Michelle. "I've something to tell you," Stephen stuttered during a heart-to-heart with this sibling. "I'm gay." He waited for the reaction. Shock, disbelief, tears? But they never came.

"Yeah," she asked, in her matter-of fact way, "And? Sure I always thought you were," she shrugged as she embraced her bemused brother.

The pair talked at length about the implications and Michelle reassured an anxious Stephen that it wouldn't change an ounce of the love his family felt for him. For Stephen, it meant that he now had a close family member to confide in, and Michelle would remain a constant force by his side as he dealt with the fallout from superstardom.

As his teen years passed by, life was not as promising for Steve Howard. Drugs were a nasty scourge that had ripped through the heart of the Sherriff Street community. And at the time the dirty brown draw of heroin was the main substance plaguing the inner city.

Howard, young and naïve, started down the slippery slope of class A drug use. "Come on Steo, would you have some fuckin' craic?" he'd ask, inviting young Gately to a local rave. But it wasn't the entertainer's scene.

Howard first started taking ecstasy tablets and then progressed to smoking heroin. He quickly became hooked, as his grip loosened on the glittering world of music and dance, and he instead chose the destructive path of an instant fix.

"Why do you do it?" a frustrated Stephen would ask his friend. "Look at what it's doing to you man. You're destroying yourself," he snapped. But he had pleaded with Howard so many times; he knew his distressed words were falling on deaf ears.

"I know Steo, I'm trying," his friend's voice trailed off. His long-time companion was beginning to look a shadow of his former self. Droopy eyelids, pasty skin, dark circles under his eyes. The kid who had become like a brother to him in this begrimed town was being sucked in between its very cracks.

And still Howard refused to give up. He had desperately tried to come off drugs on several occasions with the help of his family. But with little professional help available in Dublin in the early 90s, he was fighting a losing battle.

"He's not shooting up," local community workers told Stephen on the occasions he convinced his friend to knock on their door. "He only smokes the shit. He's not on the priority list. Come back when he injects."

For Stephen himself, music and dance were the only lifelines that helped him stay away from the dark enticements of his hometown. The most he ever experimented was with cannabis, but while his friends struck a light under an old metal spoon and let the black star seep into their veins to carry them away, the youngster had a steady head on his shoulders. Steady enough to know there were no quick fixes on his route away from Sherriff Street.

***

But then his moment came. After years of trudging through dance classes and singing auditions, the glimmer of hope that he had long been searching for finally arrived in the shape of a small newspaper advert.

Gately, now 17, was flicking through the *Evening Herald* one day when a short listing caught his eye.

WANTED: The Irish Take That: Men between the ages of 16 and 26 for an all new Irish boy band. If you can sing, dance and think you have got what it takes come down to XXX where Louis Walsh will be holding auditions.

At the time boy bands were selling out arenas all over the UK but hadn't yet reached Ireland, and Stephen instantly recognised the once-in-a-lifetime opportunity.

He had followed Take That with religious fervour. The band had been nurtured by producer Nigel Martin Smith and had enjoyed a run of chart-topping hits in the U.K. He knew a new pop group called The Backstreet Boys were also taking the United States by storm.

He'd long dreamed of being in a boy band and American groups such as Boyz II Men and New Kids on the Block had shown him the dizzying heights that young performers could reach if they had a good manager behind them and were given have a chance to shine.

Pictures of some of the bands had covered the walls of his modest bedrooms. The shiny posters of the young pop idols watched over him as he practiced his moves day in, day out, in front of his bedroom mirror.

Then of course there was the contact name. Louis Walsh. A recognised and well-liked talent spotter who had already taken the dreams of a young singer/songwriter called Johnny Logan and spun them into pure gold. Walsh had persuaded Logan to enter the 1980 Irish National Song Contest. He won and then went on to the 25th Eurovision Song Contest, where he achieved glory in front of 500 million TV viewers.

The date on the ad was a full week away but Stephen couldn't wait that long. He knew his height could hold him back from being in the band. He was only 5 foot 7 inches and not the size of the typical strapping young men being handpicked to win the hearts of hundreds and thousands of teenagers the country over.

He put the phone to his ear and dialled the number. "Hello is that Louis Walsh?" he asked, his heart now thumping in his chest. "Em…My name is Stephen Gately and I'm interested in trying out for your new band."

"Well come along then and show us what you've got," encouraged Louis with the same enthusiasm he had given his umpteenth enquirer that day.

"Yeah but how tall do ya have to be to be in Boyzone?" he quizzed. He was worried that being 5 foot 7 was too short. In later years, while auditioning for The Hobbit, Stephen would say he was 5 foot 3 and his Boyzone pals would slag him over the fact that they never really knew how tall he was.

In fact, at his funeral mass, Ronan would poignantly tell his family and friends "I don't think Stephen knew either but he was a giant of a man in our hearts."

"What height are you then Stephen," chuckled Louis, tickled at the nervous Dubliner fretting over a few inches. "Eh…5 foot 8," came his sheepish reply.

"Well look if your voice is bigger than your size we'll see what we can do," and the line went dead.

Stephen dropped the phone and breathed a sigh of relief. He was quivering with excitement at the possibility of it all. But never for a moment did he dare think that he shouldn't get his hopes up. Something deep down inside him, a little voice that had been pushing him on for all those years in the face of ridicule, told him that this was his moment to shine.

For the next few days he practised as if his life depended on it. Evening after evening the strong melodic tones of his determined voice could be heard drifting throughout the apartment and out the window of his bedroom onto the world below. Letting everyone know he meant business.

The morning of the audition, his palms sweaty, hair slicked back with more hair gel than a Robert Palmer backing dancer, he turned the corner towards the audition centre with a confident stride…until he saw his competition. The queue of young men, tall and handsome, shirts opened and bodies ripped, stretched as far as the eye could see and then around the block. Hopefuls had come – literally in their hundreds – to be in with a chance of achieving the superstardom only someone like Walsh could offer.

"Oh Fuck," he whispered to himself, before checking himself and shaking off the hesitation. "This one is yours Stephen. Just give it your best."

The army of nervous applicants were each asked to sing Careless Whisper by George Michael. Each audition would be taped and watched again to judge the applicant's performance. And, out of the 300, only 50 would be selected for the second and final round.

He felt tiny in the queue, as he pinned his number to his shirt and surveyed the crowd. How was he going to stand out? How could he become one of the 50 to be noticed and invited back?

But the moment he stood in front of Louis, little Stephen from Dublin's Sherriff Street secured his own destiny.

He was nervous at first; painfully aware of the expectant eyes taking him in. The powerful weight of the very moment hung in the air as he took a final deep breath and belted out the first notes of the song. Louis slowly sat back, being careful not to give his thoughts away. But as Stephen gave it his all, a flicker of optimism sparkled through the manager's eyes. The boy was brilliant.

Sprawled out in front of Louis were dozens of pictures of Stephen in various catalogue poses. Copies of his CV were strewn across the desk along with an amateurish tape that Stephen had pre-recorded on a stereo back home. The boy had inundated him with material showcasing his talents from the minute he received his first phone call. And Louis was in no doubt of his drive and ambition. He had outshone all of the hopefuls by a long shot with the sheer fire in his belly. But the gift that he displayed this day was utterly incredible. Louis knew immediately he was on to a winner.

As the song went on, Stephen became more confident, giving it his all as he boldly reached the climax.
"I'm never gonna dance again
guilty feet have got no rhythm
though it's easy to pretend
I know you're not a fool….."

He was in full swing now, as if he were dancing around as he always did, in the bedroom of his dingy flat.

A loud solo applause greeted the final bars of his audition.

"I like it. You've got talent kid," Louis grinned like a cat who'd lapped the cream. "You've just made my day. You're through to the next round."

Louis would later recall, "I said to myself 'this guy is going to make me a multi-millionaire'. When I looked at him I saw thousands of screaming fans. Girls waiting outside his hotel room, begging him to sign their latest piece of merchandise. As far as I was concerned he was going to break a million hearts. A ladies man through and through. I couldn't sign him quick enough."

Today he laughs at the irony of his summation. "Gay? It never even crossed my mind for a second. His baby face and big eyes were exactly what we needed to steal hearts. Stephen was going to be huge."

For the second audition the applicants were asked to sing two songs, including one of their own choice with a backing tape. Stephen paced outside as he tried to get his head in the right place.

Other hopefuls that day included Mikey Graham, who sang *Two Out of Three Ain't Bad* by Meat Loaf; Keith Duffy, who did a cringe worthy rendition of *I'm Too Sexy* by Right Said Fred and Ronan Keating who sang *Father and Son* by Cat Stevens (a cover version of which the band would later release). Stephen held his own by again singing a powerful version of George Michael's *Careless Whisper*.

Stephen stunned Louis again and before the evening fell he was called to a small room to hear the verdict.

His throat dry and knees weak, he stood before Louis knowing full well that this was his make or break moment. This would decide if he was going to be back scraping paint off walls for the rest of his life, or covering them with his official tour posters. Everything rested on this moment. His one ticket out of this Godforsaken town.

"Kid," a vivacious Louis smiled brightly as he looked him in the eye. "I'm sorry but I'm not going to make you a star," he sighed.

Stephen's heart crashed through the floor.

"I'm going to make you a superstar. You've got the job."

And with that Stephen Gately's life changed forever.

CHAPTER THREE

A Star is Born

Stephen put his head in his hands and covered his ears to block out the noise. He could feel the nerves setting in. They hadn't practised; they weren't choreographed; they hadn't even thought to coordinate their wardrobe. This was going to be an absolute disaster and a million people would be watching it unfold in their own living rooms.

A young girl wearing a headset popped her head around the door: "Five minutes lads and you're on," she called. Right this is it," said Louis springing out of his seat. "I want you to give it everything you've got. I want them to be throwing their knickers at their television sets." The boys managed a nervous laugh.

It was 1993 and the six hopeful young men had gathered backstage in the RTE television studios minutes before, anxiously awaiting their debut performance on *The Late Late Show*. Nervous tension hung in their air as the reality of the moment hit them. Boyzone were about to be unleashed onto the world.

Stephen sat looking at Louis as their mentor delivered his pep talk, praying to God he knew what he was doing. The idea that his destiny rested in the hands of this one man was almost too much to bear. Exchanging equally nervous glances were the remainder of the Boyzone line-up: Ronan Keating, Keith Duffy, Shane Lynch and two other Dubliners, Mark Walton and Richie Rock. Mark and Richie would eventually be cast aside in favour of Mikey Graham, but for now it was in the hands of these six to launch Boyzone into the big bad world of show business.

The Late Late Show host Gay Byrne gave them their cue and the lads filed out onto the stage, as Stephen tried to shake the feeling in the pit of his stomach that they were about to be thrown to the sharks. This was the moment he had dreamed of – but it wasn't supposed to be like this. It was supposed to be their big break, but somehow it was beginning to feel more like a ritual humiliation.

"Now ladies and gentlemen, these lads have decided to cash in on a particular market," said the presenter. "Can I please introduce you to Ireland's answer to Take That."

As the audience tried to work out what the band actually brought to the table, Gay had a great time explaining their skills – or lack thereof.

"There's no talent whatsoever. Nothing. They don't sing, they don't write music and they don't play instruments."

It was painful. Stephen winced, as he wondered what he had let himself in for. He had gone through years of performing arts classes, and for what? He was about make a complete fool of himself in front of the entire nation. The only thing he could think of was his mother, sitting, watching at home.

"I'm a pianist," Stephen piped up in a thick Dublin accent. "A what?" The crowd was already in stitches. "A pianist," he stressed.

But his coarse brogue corrupted the word again and the crowd were baying like hyenas.

One by one Gay asked the group to call out their names and where they were from for the viewers. Stephen felt like a nervous schoolboy on the first term's roll call. When it came to his turn to speak he tried to blurt out the name of his street, but his thin voice was barely audible. The audience burst into fits of laughter.

Once more Stephen felt his cheeks flare up. He was all too familiar with the reaction that any mention of his address provoked. The moment you mentioned it in a job interview, you could kiss your prospects goodbye. And yet here he was in front of millions of viewers telling them where he was from and expecting them to believe that he wasn't just as good as them, but that one day he was going to even bigger than they could ever imagine.

Did he even half believe in himself? Perhaps that's why the words stuck in his dry throat under the bright studio lights. Maybe he didn't belong here after all. This was supposed to be the end of the beginning, but already it felt more like the beginning of the end. He would have to do something.

The bemused crowd giggled on, until Gay decided it was best to get on with the hanging and cued the backing track: *Burn Baby Burn*. Suddenly, the beat kicked in and Stephen – who was standing at the end of the line looking painfully shy – virtually leapt out of his skin as the opening bars sounded. He realised this was his moment to shine. It was now or never. After all, he had nothing to lose.

Twirling like a dervish in front of the others, he stopped dead centre stage before pulling back his brown waistcoat and opening his white shirt to reveal a scrawny white chest underneath. The audience roared with laughter. But he danced on, unfazed by the cynics. Behind him, with little evidence of anything resembling choreography, shirts were flung open, as his fellow bandmates pranced around the studio.

A bare-chested Shane Lynch, in a pair of pale blue denim dungarees, caused a commotion when he grabbed his crotch just inches from the front row of the audience. The crowd yelped in a mixture of excitement and shock. The boys played up to the fuss, each knowing that none of them had a clue what they were supposed to be doing. Ronan and Stephen took to the foreground, giving it all they had, and eventually stole the limelight. It was a cringe worthy routine, but ironically, it would set the tone for the boys who were to emerge as the two brightest stars in the band for many years to come.

"Right lads, thank you and good luck to you," the tickled presenter said as he shooed them off stage. "We look forward to hearing from you when you're famous." Was it a nice sentiment, or was it sarcasm? One thing was sure: nobody in the studio that night believed it, or realised how prophetic those words would prove to be.

For two months after *The Late Late Show* shambles, the band travelled around Ireland in a battered old Transit van, dodging bottles and other missiles from fans who weren't impressed with their unrefined show. As Stephen and the boys put their heart into routines in front of near-empty halls, the few onlookers who had bothered to gather would flick cigarette butts their way and laugh them off the stage.

"Get off the fucking stage," they'd shout. "Who the fuck are ya? Take That's pikey cousins?"

"This is shite," groaned Stephen as he came off after another painful performance. "Is this what it's all about? I'd make more money scraping shite off walls for me da'. That bottle nearly hit me that time too, the fucking prick."

The lads tried to keep their spirits up by making light of the situation. "We should call it The Doorstep Tour," they quipped. "Sure the stages that we've to perform on are hardly any bigger."

In fact there were many occasions where the boys would pack into the van and travel hundreds of miles across Ireland only to discover that the "nightclub" they were performing in was actually the extension of somebody's house.

"What the fuck?" cried Stephen as they arrived at one such venue. "You've got to be taking the piss? Sure if I wanted to be singing in a place this size I could've stayed at home singing into my fucking bedroom mirror. And I'd probably be paid more."

The boys cracked up. For all the complaining they remained unbowed. They would dance on tables. Play in small villages in the middle of nowhere, travel day and night to make sure that every corner of Ireland knew their name. If they captured only ten fans for the sake of a 200 mile round trip it would be worth it.

On the other side of the water, Take That were ruling the boy band circuit. There was rarely a day that would go by that Boyzone wouldn't listen to the radio in their cramped van as the chart topping hits of Robbie Williams, Gary Barlow, Howard Donald, Jason Orange and Mark Owen rang out from the speakers.

Sometimes they sang along, but after long days on the road with little thanks, they would sit in silence listening enviously, wishing that they too were household names. Huddled in their clapped-out van, travelling to venues no one outside of Ireland had ever heard of, they felt a million miles away from the international stardom they craved.

But all that was about to change. Louis Walsh had been busy putting the first steps in place. The boys had been summoned to a small Dublin studio early one morning in early 1994 to record their first single.

Stephen took a final glance in the bathroom mirror and tweaked his heavily gelled hair to perfection before heading out the door. It was a big day for him and he wanted to look the part. He felt like the epitome of cool strutting into the studio for the first time, and swung the door open to find all the boys had the same idea. They had thrown on their best threads for the occasion and even Shane and Keith, who were trying to appear as if they were taking it all in their stride, reeked of a couple of young boys who were desperate to impress. They all did.

"Right let's get cracking," Louis said, clapping his hands as he power walked into the room and introduced them to the producer.

The lads piled into the small studio behind him, stealing a few sly glances at the giant intimidating mixing desk that sat before them. Some of them began shyly trying out buttons on the soundboard, curiously flicking the master controls.

"Leave that to the professional lads," Louis chuckled, slapping away their hand. "One step at a time."

"Ok here's how it's going to be," he continued, while handing out sheets of lyrics. "Mikey and Stephen come over here beside me. You're going to be my two main singers."

Stephen jumped up with a mixture of enthusiasm and awkwardness as the others looked on, visibly wounded by the remark. Ronan in particular appeared more put out than the others. He had been warming up his vocals all morning and believed he had one of the strongest voices in the group. He decided to bite his lip for the moment. Surely he would be given his lines as the day wore on.

But, as the hours ticked by, and Stephen and Mikey sang their lines a thousand times over, tension began growing in the room. The duo had been tutored about breathing and timing and strength of voice, as sighs from the rest of the group grew louder. They looked at each other quietly across the room, wondering who was going to speak up first.

Eventually one of them piped up: "This is bullshit, Louis. When are we going to get our chance?"

"Trust me I know what I'm doing," he reassured them. "When you're all being chased by screaming girls and making lots of money you won't have any complaints," he shrugged.

By the end of the day, in the midst of take-aways and empty cans of coke, they wrapped up a successful day of recording. *Working My Way Back to You* was pumping out the speakers and sounding good. Louis, Stephen and Mikey bobbed their head along to the beat as the others listened on, a lot more insecure than when they had first walked through the studio door.

A few days later they all received the first pressed copy in their hands. Stephen put it to his nose and took a deep breath, "Maaan, I can't believe it. We've finally done it," he laughed.

When the record hit the shops he walked by the windows to see a picture of the band in white t-shirts and baseball caps smiling back at him on the cover of the new track. He stood laughing before calling Louis. After a couple of attempts, his manager called him back.

"Where the hell have you been," he asked his boss. "Have you seen it yet?"

"Of course I've seen it," chuckled Louis. "Sure, aren't I staring at a couple of hundred copies in the boot of my car?"

The shrewd music mogul had done what any reasonable band manager would do and bought them all up. "I'm going to get you guys in the top ten, if it breaks me," he announced, before hanging up the phone.

His dedication paid off. The single sailed up the charts to number four. The lads were elated, hugging and clapping each other on the back before Louis burst their bubble.

"Of course you're number four," he reasoned, "sure I bought up half the damn things. You're going to have to do a lot better than that if you want to make it in this business," he warned.

Still, people were beginning to take notice. They were gradually being recognized more and more on the street and teenage girl fans were following their every move. One day after an umpteenth public performance, Stephen was making his way back to the van when he heard someone shout "Stephen, STEPHEN!"

How many times had he walked down the street and start to run as soon as he heard his name yelled out? But this time it was different. There were no taunts or jibes. Just a louder, more pleading tone. "Steeeephen, any chance of an autograph?"

His heart stopped. And the beginnings of a smile crept across his baby face. He had waited so long for this moment. Suddenly it was worth the all-night road trips, the dingy halls, the constant feeling of loneliness on his many months away from home.

He spun round. A young girl, perhaps not even yet a teenager, stood timidly with her hand outstretched. He took the marker and laughed, "Yeah sure, who should I make it out to?" With a flick of his pen, he signed his name. The autograph he'd practiced a thousand times over, but this time it was for real. And God it felt good.

As their popularity rose, Stephen and Ronan began attracting most of the attention from fans. The other guys saw this and it brought tension as they toured Ireland, cramped together, for months at a time. To make matters worse, Walsh threw his hat into the mix with straight-talking comments about the rest of the band. "The other lads are 'passengers' in the group," he was heard saying one day. A fight broke out and egos had to be briskly massaged.

"We all play a part. Every fucking last one of us," they argued. "There'd be no band if you didn't have the rest of us. Just because you're not pushing us up front with vocals. You barely give us half a chance."

But Stephen didn't need to worry. He was, in his own right, making his mark. His name would often be called along with Ronan's by the rapidly growing loyal following of fans who would wait until all hours just to get a snap with their teenage crush. Everywhere they went, outside venues, as they climbed into waiting cars; there they would be, patient as ever, in the hope of stealing some precious time with Ireland's new boy band stars star. Pen in hand, pleading for a signature, a kiss, anything that would give them a moment with the heartthrob whose picture adorned their bedroom walls.

"Fucking hell lads," Stephen laughed. "I've just been on to home. They're knocking on me ma's door at all hours looking for me. Pity they didn't do it when I fucking lived there," he laughed. He picked up one of the pairs of knickers thrown on stage and playfully threw them over his pal's head. "Get a load of that," he chuckled.

Ronan piped up: "I don't care what you say, it ain't any of us Steo; the girls all love you. Yeah we get our share, but do you see them when you do the live gigs man? The place completely erupts. There's no denying that."

And he was right. As that stage, Stephen was receiving thousands of fan letters a week as well as being mobbed by hundreds of love-hungry girls.

"It's fantastic," Stephen would laugh after clawing his way through the mob, "Scares the shit outta me but good for the ego."

He was still keeping the secret of his sexuality under wraps and even his band mates didn't know he was gay. As the group's fame spread across Ireland, Stephen was main attraction. With his baby faced looks and cute smile, he played up to the fans every fantasy as he sang sweetly into their eyes.

In fact Walsh had already dreamed up the perfect marketing ploy to appeal to the pre-teens.

The group combined their laid back Irish charm with boyish good looks, and their five distinctive personalities worked together to create something utterly unique. And it was something their manager wanted to cash in on.

"Right lads you're all virgins, got it?" The boys nearly choked with laughter.

"You what?" they scoffed in utter disbelief.

"You heard me, if you want to sell records; you've got to appeal to the dreams of young teenage girls. You can't be spotted with your hand up some mini-skirt at three in the morning on the way home from a nightclub. That'll ruin the image. So here's the way it is; you're all saving yourselves for 'the one'. For the right girl to come along, you got it?"

"Your mothers are the only women in your life," he finished as they all cracked up with laughter. But they knew he was thinking of the bigger picture – and money.

And when Louis Walsh was in that frame of mind he meant business.

***

It wasn't until the winter of 1994 that Boyzone began to make it big across the water in the U.K. After the success of their earlier hits, Walsh had quickly realised their ticket to fame.

Artistic independence was not vital to win success. The key was to perform covers of well-liked but widely forgotten '70s pop tunes. The younger generation didn't know the songs and if they were a hit before, they'd sail up to the top of the charts again. "If it's not broken, don't fix it," explained Louis.

He had gathered them around to give them the big news. "I've got the single that's going to make your name in the UK," he announced. "Trust me – this is going to make you huge."

He put the record on play and sat back, thrilled with himself as The Osmonds' *Love Me for a Reason* filled the room. It was perfect.

It gave Boyzone their chart breakthrough in Britain, where the record soared to number two, only deprived of the top spot by the less well-heeled boys from East Seventeen, who had pocketed the coveted number one with their Christmas anthem *Stay Another*

Day.

They toured radio stations, performed concert after concert and worked around the clock to make sure every teenage girl had a Boyzone single in their CD stand and a Boyzone poster on their wall. Instead of playing on doorstep stages in Limerick they were now performing in front of hundreds of people.

Their merchandise knew no bounds. Posters, coffee cups, coasters, school bags, toothbrushes, pencils, t-shirts, key-rings and even Boyzone car fresheners. And it all was adding up to a big pay day.

***

With their increasing fame, came mounting pressures and Stephen began to find it more and more difficult to keep his sexuality under wraps. Some of the other guys would sneak female fans back to their hotel rooms to curb the lonely nights on the road. He would often hear the giggling and partying in the room next door as he sat up in bed watching movies, trying to tire himself out before he drifted off to sleep.

How long could he keep this up? They were constantly asking questions and even though the bands had to pretend they were virgins to the outside world, he had no excuse not to be pulling a different girl every night, as far as the lads were concerned.

"Well did you get your bit last night Steo?," one of his bandmates would innocently enquire as Stephen settled into the tour van, pulling a baseball cap down over his face, trying to hide his exhaustion and nurse a hangover brought on by the night before.

They weren't to know, but their gentle questioning sent his pulse racing every time their curiosity got the better of them. "No, I was shattered, I just hit the sack," he replied, trying to end the conversation.

"Steo, man you're only young once. There are hundreds of girls screaming your name. Gagging for your babies. Take your pick mate. The world is your fucking oyster." What more do you want them to do? They're fucking throwing themselves at you? It's not like you even have to chat them up."

It soon became apparent that Stephen couldn't keep brushing them off. Even for himself more than anyone, he wanted to believe that he was into women, for his career. He had to keep up the act. His image was built on a lie and if he let it slip his whole career would come crashing down. The easiest thing to do was to bed a couple of girls. How bad could it be? He hated the thought of it but a couple of drinks in his system and he was prepared to give it a shot.

It was only years later, backstage at the Irish Meteor Music Awards, that a finally outed Stephen Gately admitted to me the lengths he would go to in order to protect his long-held secret. Ironically he was sitting beside Andy Cowles at the time, his husband and the love of his life, who remained with him till the day he died.

In a candid interview he described how he slept with several young female fans in order to live up to the heartthrob image.

"Oh man," he said jokingly putting his head in his hands. "What was I thinking? At the time it just felt like it was the only option. It was like I had boxed myself into an image or a way of life and that was my lot. I just had to get on with it. The poor girls. As far as I was concerned, I couldn't have got it over with quick enough," Cowles laughed beside him.

"Shut up!" he said, playfully slapping his thigh. It wasn't fucking funny. I remember kicking them out of the hotel room as soon as it was over. They would give me their number on a torn up piece of paper. It was embarrassing for them; it was obvious I wasn't interested. I felt so bad. And a lot of the time I couldn't bring myself to…you know…get it up," he winced. "I couldn't even do the job. Well what would you expect?" he laughed. "I just blamed the demon drink. It was an experience, I'll put it that way," he offered with a pained expression on his face. "Let's just leave it at that."

Ironically in a strange twist of fate he quickly added, "don't write any of what I said." He was trying to keep his heterosexual dalliances under wraps. How the tables had turned.

Back then however, he didn't have such a light-hearted approach. And he needed some of his old friends around to keep him in touch with reality. Even if they weren't in a good place themselves at the time.

One such friend was his childhood buddy Stephen Howard.

***

As Stephen's fame grew, Steve Howard was more and more often on the scene. But Walsh wasn't having any of it. He would constantly tell the singer he had reached the big time and in order to stay there he would need to break away from negative influences in his life.

"Get him out of here," ordered Louis, when the Boyzone singer organised backstage passes for Howard to attend to their gigs. "I don't want him around. He's not good for you Stephen. If you're serious about your career then cut out all of the shit."

"Sorry man, manager's orders," an uncomfortable Stephen would tell his friend as he shrugged apologetically at the stage door.

"Ah for fuck sake Steo, we're just hanging out. You're forgetting about your old mates already are you?" Howard snapped before turning on his heel. "Fuck this, I don't need you anyway," he spat as he walked into the night.

It would be one of the last times the two boys met. Howard hanged himself years later on the staircase of his home. He was only 21.

Later friends would recall how Stephen's first childhood friend never got over the hurt of being rejected. "Howard could never understand why he was being frozen out. The two of them had been inseparable for years and suddenly Steve was not allowed to hang around with Gately or the rest of the band.

"Louis would order him out if he saw him. Other friends would get tickets for events but not Steve Howard. It really hurt him."

It was only after his death that a broken hearted Gately dedicated a Boyzone record to his friend. A small but touching acknowledgement at the part he had played in igniting his passion for music and dance.

***

It was now 1995 and Take That were heading for a high profile split. Boyzone saw their chance to become Britain's Number one boy band. A Polydor Records representative had offered Walsh €100,000 for the first three Boyzone singles and an album and he grabbed the opportunity with both hands.

The boys were finally about to see the big bucks roll in. They just didn't realise how far they were going to be propelled towards the dizzying heights of fame and fortune. Indeed Polydor would later discover they had just landed the pop bargain of the decade. Soon, the lads were sweeping the pop awards and a string of Top 10 hits confirmed their position as the UK's favourite boy band.

It would prove to be a huge year for Stephen and the band. *Said and Done* crashed into the UK number one spot. *Key to My Life* peaked at number three, as did their hit single *So Good*, while the classic *Father and Son* reached number two. It seemed like everything they touched turned to gold and the boys with the Midas touch could start living a life they had never dreamed possible.

In the excitement, Stephen felt he never really got time to let the madness of it all sink in. One day he was waiting with baited breath to see if they had secured the coveted number one spot, the next he was told to pack his suitcase as he was on a plane to the Far East. Before he could blink he was thousands of miles from home, plugging the album to fans in an exotic land before jetting off again to the next far flung country.

There were days when he woke up and he didn't even know where he was. Often, when he called his mother back home, he had to stop and think where he was when she asked. His body clock was a mess. And as for record sales? He didn't even know anymore. He was at full throttle just trying to keep pace with the whirlwind of fame.

At the same time however, he was having the time of his life. He was seeing places he had never even heard of, albeit through the window of a bus to and from the airport, but he was gaining experience beyond his wildest dreams.

"We had so much fun," Stephen laughed as he recalled his time on the road. "That was the key to it lasting for so long, because a lot of boy bands don't last as long as we did. I have to say, it was mostly good and happy when we were together, and that's pretty unusual."

***

As the happy times rolled in, so too did the money. Stephen's first ever cheque had been for the princely sum of £8,000, after a year and a half of blood, sweat and tears – and now the figures were getting bigger and bigger all the time. He had held it aloft like a trophy, brought it down to his lips and kissed it like it was his first child. "God that feels good," he laughed. "That's what it's all about lads. We've fucking earned it."

He bought designer clothes, albums, things for home and flittered it away because he knew there was plenty more where that came from. The singer couldn't drive at the time so while the others were splashing out on flash motors, he was investing in something more lasting.

When the Boyzone phenomenon was in full swing, one of his big first purchases was a mansion in Newtownmountkennedy, Co Wicklow, The old mill house was owned by a family called the Dixons, and Gately bought it for €550,000. With the help of his brother-in-law, architect Alan Carr, he worked hard on renovating it, making it his dream home.

"I've found the perfect place", he would tell the band. "It's like something out of a Disney movie. It's surrounded by these majestic trees, and to get up to it you have to go up a long winding driveway; it's in the middle of nowhere too. The perfect getaway from all this madness."

For a while during his stay, residents of the village became familiar with the sight of his long suffering fans, who travelled by bus to catch a glimpse of their hero. Unfortunately for them, Gately generally remained beyond the gates, seldom venturing out.

However it wasn't long before he wanted to move onto greener pastures and he put the house on the market, making €100,000 profit on its sale. Before he left however, he used it as a backdrop for a photo shoot in *OK magazine*.

It was only in later years that Gately would discover he had lost out on €2.5 million by selling before Ireland's property boom kicked in. It was a lot of money, even by Boyzone's sell out concert standards, but he didn't wallow in the loss for too long.

Boyzone get the street look in 1995 in one of their early publicity shoots in London.

Before they hit the big time
- Stephen would look back on their tacky early photo shoots and cringe.

The humble family home on Sheriff Street where Stephen said 'We didn't have lots of money but it was a real family home.'

Stephen's first love Stephen Howard who took his own life. Depressed Stephen Howard couldn't kick heroin after he and Stephen split.

Life is a roller coaster. Stephen gives the thumbs up as he helped launch the Playstation ride at Blackpool Pleasure beach - alongside 94-year old thrill seeker Doris Thompson.

Stephen gets into the Christmas spirit in 1997 with his band mates.

official calendar 1997

Fancy a date? Stephen was typically the centre of attention when Boyzone released their money spinning calender in 2007 which was a huge hit despite their garish outfits.

Stephen's first big acting gig was with legendary Rowan Atkinson when the Blackadder star agreed to appear in their pop video for A Picture Of You.

Stephen was destined for the West End even before he landed his first role in Joseph. The singer relished the chance of meeting Andrew Lloyd Webber with his band mates in 1998. Webber would hand him the coveted lead role in Joseph years later.

Stephen gets in the spirit when he pulls on a red nose with Victoria Wood and band mate Keith Duffy for Comic Relief in 1999.

Mum's the word. Stephen's mum Margeret joined the army of Boyzone fans as the star's fame hit dazzling heights in 1999.

Singing for the victims - Stephen and Ronan belt out a hit during a concert to raise money for the Omagh bomb families.

The front page that broke a million female hearts. Stephen's shock announcement was front page news all over the world in June 1999.

A man in demand, Stephen had no shortage of product endorsement offers in 1999 as he enjoyed the heights of fame with Boyzone.

The romance that rocked the showbiz world: Stephen and his boyfriend Eloy were never far from a paparazzi lens as their relationship hit the headlines.

I'll drink to that! Stephen takes time out at the end of 2000 to enjoy a water in the Devonshire Hotel as he launched his solo album.

Friends in high places - Stephen pictured with Elton John
and David Furnish leaving the Old Vic Benefit concert in Waterloo.

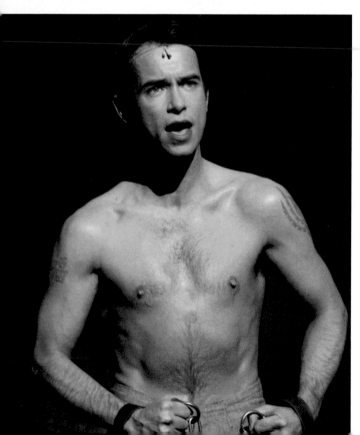

Chained to his
new life on the
stage - Stephen
was a big hit as
Joseph when he
landed the role in
2003.

My 2004 front page exclusive which exposed the huge rift between the Boyzone members which lead to their split and stood in the way of a comeback tour.

The singer landed another big West End role in 2004 when he
played the Evil Child Catcher in Chitty Chitty Bang Bang.

"No point on making it if you don't enjoy it lads", he lamented afterwards, "and I have many a good memory from there."

The important thing for Stephen was that he loved what he was doing. He had come so far from breaking his back with hard labour scraping the paint from the walls of Dublin homes. And he was literally earning thousands of times more. What more could he ask for? He was living the dream.

***

But the Boyzone bubble didn't stop him being exposed to the impoverished side of life and a trip to Bangkok hammered home the privilege of their situation.

When they landed in the capital of Thailand, the poverty knocked them for six. As they lived it up in their plush five star accommodations, the ramshackle communities of wooden shacks around them made for an unsettling wake up call.

"I want to give something back lads," he told the others. "I'm finding it hard to get my head around how lucky we've all been, you know? And I'm not going to let the opportunity to do some good pass me by." They all agreed. And one by one they began to pick individual charities in keeping with their promise.

For his part Stephen went on to become a vice patron of the charity Missing People, supporting their Runaway Helpline service for young people. He also dedicated much of his free time to the Caudwell Children Charity based in Stoke-on-Trent, ironically the home town of a certain Robbie Williams.

The big hearted Gately, who was known for his secretive hospital visits, would arrive unannounced to spend some time with his sick fans. On one such occasion he met a child who fell in love with his jacket. Gately allowed her to try it on. "Go on, you have it," he offered. "It looks better on you." The girl gave a faint smile as he chatted for a while to her parents while she dozed off in the background.

An hour later he was in the car driving back to his hotel when his phone rang. It was the hospital to say the little girl had passed away shortly after he left. Stephen dropped the phone and cried the whole way home.

***

It was late 1996 and the boys still had a rollercoaster ride ahead of them. They were already proving they were going to be one of the biggest boy bands ever to grace the planet when they went on to achieve their first UK number one hit with *Words*.

They were on top of the world. Working with four best mates, jumping on planes and travelling to far flung countries, living in the best hotels and singing in front of audiences of up to 100,000 people. It couldn't get much better than this! As the group partied into the night, popping the champagne and hugging each other in the midst of boozy heart-to-hearts, little did they know that it was just the start of a fame they could never have imagined.

In total, 13 consecutive top five singles lined the path to their record smashing future in pop as *A Different Beat* and *Isn't It a Wonder* took the UK by storm. And they hadn't just conquered Britain. The group were also releasing smash hit singles as far afield as Australia and New Zealand.

"We're the luckiest bastards on the planet. Aren't we?" laughed Stephen as he hugged his bandmates, all a little the worse for drink. "We're on a one way ticket to fucking superstardom. And it just keeps getting better and better."

But Stephen was about to learn that success is a double edged sword. And it was only a matter of time until he discovered the downside to reaching the giddy heights of being an A-list celebrity and international superstar.

CHAPTER FOUR
The Day that Shook Showbiz

"If there's a place on this planet that we could go to and not be recognised, then I'd love to know where it is," Stephen Gately told me over a glass of wine one evening in 1996.

I had just asked the singer if there was anywhere he felt he could escape from the pressures of Boyzone mania, now a global phenomenon. Stephen felt both blessed and terrified by the level of super stardom the band had achieved. A flurry of number one singles and sell out tours had propelled them to a new level of adulation amongst young female pop fans who pinned their every hope and dream on the quintet.

When Take That announced that they were splitting in 1996, Boyzone's opportunistic manager Louis Walsh was quick to strike and rebrand Boyzone as the new heartthrobs of the pop world. Fundamental to his plans to cash in on the glaring void that was left by Gary Barlow and his bandmates was Stephen. As the cutesy bright-eyed pin-up, Louis convinced himself that Stephen, rather than Ronan, would carry the band forward on a wave of teenage angst and puppy love.

"It's not rocket science," Louis would tell their record label bosses during long six-hour meetings staged to plot Boyzone's rise to the summit of the charts. "Go to any of our gigs and the girls are all waving Stephen banners. I've seen with my own eyes how they stand outside his hotel every night screaming until dawn. Stephen is every teen girl's dream and we have to let them believe that there's even a minuscule chance that they can have him."

The female devotees lined up in the hundreds to mob Stephen wherever he travelled. He would frequently have to change hotel rooms in the middle of the night because the noise of screaming hoards chanting and singing to him outside his room would keep him awake until all hours. Fans would organise complex networks amongst themselves to communicate where Stephen was staying, flying to or flying from. They would even receive tip-offs about where he was heading for lunch and scramble to set up camp outside whichever posh eatery he was frequenting.

"He was virtually a prisoner of his own fame at that stage," remarked Louis. "All the lads had to deal with a lot of attention but Stephen was just followed everywhere. Boyzone mania was something they couldn't just turn on and off at will."

During their early years, members of the band claimed they did not have girlfriends, but that image was shattered when it was revealed that Mikey Graham and Keith Duffy had both become dads. Ever since then the band has been keen to extol the virtues of family life. Duffy and his girlfriend Lisa Smith had a two-year-old son, Jordan, while Graham had a two-year-old daughter with his girlfriend Sharon Keane. Meanwhile, Blond bombshell Ronan's pronouncements concerning his sex life bordered on puritanical when he announced that he was still a virgin and would remain so until marriage.

The concept was simple but effective. Stephen would be moved into a more prominent position in the group, giving him more vocals and air time in the moody, loved-up videos designed to woo an army of new female fans, heartbroken and lost since the split of Take That. For Stephen it was a crippling compromise for a man beginning, at the age of 20, to embrace, albeit privately, his own sexuality. But he was no fool. Stephen had worked his whole life for the fame and fortune he was now relishing, and he was not about to throw it away just to write his name into the history books as pop's first openly gay boy band member.

A plan was formatted with Louis and the rest of the band to cover up his true sexuality and exploit his heartthrob image. He continued dutifully singing his soulful love songs about girls and romantic crushes and he'd live up to the act by blowing air kisses to his female fans wherever he travelled. It was the perfect cover-up and one that Stephen was happy to play along with, so long as the number one singles and sell out concerts continued. Stephen would even master the art of dodging awkward questions about girls in his interviews so he could keep up the guise. As a matter of pride, he never technically lied, instead using gender-neutral terms when describing the "girl" he supposedly hoped to meet.

"When people would ask me about my favourite girls," Stephen said, "I'd describe men that I fancied – blue eyes, brown hair, whatever. I always said, 'the right person', never 'the girl'. But I used to be so paranoid that people would work it out. I'd be down in the dumps, being in the public eye for six years and always having to explain why I didn't have a girlfriend."

It was during one of my first assignments as a young showbiz columnist for the Irish Sunday Mirror that I first saw the Louis Walsh PR machine in full force. Louis' philosophy in those early days of Boyzone was simple. "If you say something enough times then it becomes true." And the celebrity-hungry tabloids were more than happy to lap up his tall tales if it meant an easy front page scoop that would sell bucket loads of newspapers.

On a Friday morning the *Sunday Mirror's* London editor called me to ask if I could use my sway with Louis to land a big Boyzone story. The equation was simple – boy band hunks sold newspapers and the formula was one the music mogul was more than happy to feed if it meant more priceless publicity for his young stars.

I called up Louis who, by the sound of the slamming breaks and beeping horns in the background, was negotiating a busy Dublin street as he weaved through traffic at breakneck speed while dreaming up a killer line for Sunday's paper. "I have one story for you, but it's a big one," he said, pausing momentarily to catch his breath. "It's about Stephen and....Baby Spice."

There was only one thing bigger than Boyzone in the pop world in 1998 and that was The Spice Girls. Their album sales made mincemeat of any of their rivals – including Louis' group. So in a crafty move which could have been straight out of a PR master class, he decided "If you can't beat them, join them".

To Louis the plan made perfect sense. While Victoria Beckham, Geri Halliwell and Mel B had all been linked to celebrities in their own right, Baby Spice Emma Bunton was still tantalisingly single, carefully protecting her bankable image as the adorable sweetheart of the girl band who wasn't quite ready to take that first big step into an adult relationship.

The excitement in Louis' voice increased a notch as his mind went into overdrive. "I'm telling you this but you have to use it big because this is a big, big story," he insisted. I was happy to oblige. "Baby Spice and Stephen have been secretly dating. They are crazy about each other and even went on a date to the theatre the other night."

It didn't take a brain surgeon to work out that the pairing of two of pop's most idolised stars was a mouth-watering match made in heaven. In fact, it existed only in Louis' imagination. But it acted as a perfect curve ball for Louis to throw into the mix as rumours within the music industry began to emerge that Stephen was not the love-hungry heterosexual star portrayed to the public.

Even if the press were gagging to out Stephen, they knew they would be taking a gamble. Without an outright confession from the man himself or a believable kiss-and-tell from an irate ex-lover, the singer's secret would be safe from the prying eyes of the press. In the meantime, they were more than happy to soak up whatever anecdotes and tall tales PR whizzes and music managers could dream up to keep the band on everyone's agenda.

The Baby Spice stunt had worked a treat. By that Sunday it was on the front pages and everyone was talking about the new romance that seemed to be made in heaven. The only problem was that Louis had forgotten to tell Stephen. "It was a total surprise to me," he said a few months later. "I didn't know anything about it and suddenly every photographer and reporter in the land was following me around to see if I would pop up somewhere with Baby Spice."

Stephen would laugh it all off with his bandmates, but privately the antics were just adding to the deluge of pressure and secrecy of what was now fast becoming a double life. For every story that leaked linking him to the latest pretty girl of the moment, the singer would feel more pressure on his shoulders.

"Sometimes I didn't even know what the truth was myself, that's how ridiculous it had become," said Stephen. "People would be asking me 'How are things going with this girl or that girl?' and I'd have to try to remember who I was meant to be seeing. To be honest it was funny at the start but it didn't take long until it started getting to me. Things like those so-called links between me and Emma Bunton. We were just mates, but when you're seen going for a drink with someone, you get seen as a couple. When a story would break with Emma or some girl then it would certainly take the pressure off for a while."

For Emma Bunton's part the story was equally baffling, "I had gotten on well with Stephen and we had been at the same event a couple of times but that was the height of it," she said. "I didn't know he was gay at the time and it wasn't any of my business. But there was certainly no dating or anything like that. Stephen never even tried to chat me up."

Stephen had turned on the tap that would drip feed every newspaper and magazine in the land. And like it or not, he knew he couldn't just turn it off when the glaring secrets and lies became too much to bare.

"Think of the fans," his close friends would tell him. "All of those girls who have invested their hopes and dreams in you – they will be crushed and they will think you cheated them." Those words would send a chill through Stephen's body. Unlike many in the showbiz scene who protested undying loyalty and love for their fans, the singer was the real deal and cringed at the thought of upsetting the millions of girls who had helped him escape his humble upbringings on Sheriff Street and live out all his wildest dreams.

"The bigger the band got the more I felt like a fraud," he would recall. "It was a monster that was getting out of control. Louis was doing what everyone thought was right for me. He was taking the heat off my private life by putting a more acceptable and bankable version of events into the public domain."

But like it or not, the blue touch paper had been lit in spectacular style. On the back of the Baby Spice "revelations" Gately was being linked to a stable of sexy females and the make believe stories about his rampant heterosexuality were growing wilder and more out of control by the day.

For the girls he was linked with it was a win-win situation. They were unlikely to object to the tidal wave of publicity such stories would attract. Being linked with one of the most eligible men in the pop world would guarantee the kind of front covers, speculation and attention money simply couldn't buy. Those girls who were the subject of the candid love links would lap up the attention, refusing to confirm or deny the rumours and allowing the speculation to go into overdrive.

On a frosty January Sunday morning in 1999 Gately awoke to read that he was about to be married to Ireland's hottest new pop sensation, a brunette beauty named Kerri-Ann. Millions of his dedicated fans must have sobbed into their cornflakes when they set eyes on the tale of the star's new love emblazoned across the *Sunday People* front page with the confident headline: *Boyzone Stephen to Marry.*

The revelations, not surprisingly, had Louis' fingerprints all over it. Since 1998 he had been helping 20 year old Kerri launch a pop career, but she had struggled to break beyond the borders of Ireland and had only minimal success. In Ireland, her first single, the salsa-tinged *Do You Love Me Boy?*, reached number two. Her follow up, *Irreplaceable*, went one better in her homeland to number one, but after being delayed a few times, the single was never released in the UK, though it did chart on import, reaching a less than spectacular 163 in the charts.

As interest waned in his girl star at the beginning of the new year, he pulled in the big guns in a last desperate bid to make her more appealing to a mass UK market.

Again the buck stopped with Stephen. He was the obvious choice for Louis to script the latest cameo appearance by a Boyzone star in a female celebrity's love life. There were few other options since his bandmates Mikey, Ronan, Keith and Shane were all in serious relationships. Again, it's unlikely Stephen knew anything about the story before it hit the front pages. And by the time it did, their pseudo romance was almost believable.

"Stephen has finally joined his other Boyzone bandmates and found true love," the article announced, before telling how "pals" of the singer were in little doubt that Kerri-Ann was the woman of his dreams."They just click and they want to settle down and get married. It will happen within the next six months."

Another splurge of romance rumours followed. When he was pictured hugging Boyzone Magazine editor Allison Maud, conclusions were readily drawn with little regard for the truth. "I was hugging Stephen, not kissing him," she protested after being hunted down by the *Mail on Sunday*. "I'm definitely not his girlfriend." But still they stirred it up: "Will all those hearts be broken now Stephen has found true love?" they asked. "Stunned fans spotted the chart-topping singer kissing a mystery girl during filming of the band's new video at Glasgow Airport."

Next in line was was the stunning Miss Scotland Isla Sutherland, who had captured Stephen's heart to such a degree that he flew her to Dublin to meet his family – as far as the newspapers were concerned anyway. In truth, Isla had bumped into the Boyzone lads at an event in Dublin and ended up enjoying a few drinks with them. She had hit it off with Stephen and they spent around 20 minutes chatting in a bar. But by the time tales of their rendezvous a deux had reached the pages of the tabloids sources were telling how he was so smitten that they had taken a tour of his home city and dropped in to visit the entire Gately clan.

***

Stephen reluctantly embraced the never-ending stream of tales and titillation about his private life. Not least because, behind the polished exterior of his squeakily clean boy band persona, the singer who had been linked to some of the celebrity world's prettiest women was in reality beginning to develop his first serious relationship with a man – Dutch pop star Eloy de Jong.

To Stephen's bandmates his sexuality was never shrouded in the secrecy and deception which had now become part of the norm for his public persona. "Stephen would have his boyfriends sitting around drinking with us while we sat with our girlfriends," Ronan recalled. "We were all 100 per cent cool with it. We always backed Stephen and it was just normality to us."

However, with Eloy – a popular 24 year old singer who enjoyed considerable fame and wealth of his own with the group Caught in the Act – Stephen knew it was more than just a fleeting romance. They had struck up a friendship after running into each other at the countless music awards ceremonies and festivals around Europe. But it took several years for their love to blossom.

"I remember knowing he was gay from the first time I met him, and he knew the same about me," Stephen would later say. "But that didn't mean we were automatically ready to jump into a relationship with each other. We had a lot in common. We had been in the public eye from a young age, and we both had to keep our sexuality a secret. We just clicked but it was some time before the spark of love was ignited."

Eloy was the perfect remedy for Stephen, who at the age of 20 had still not found his feet in a confident way to enjoy the comfort of a mature relationship. Eloy, on the other hand, was larger than life – both physically and in spirit. He didn't labour under a constant strain of guilt or paranoia over his sexuality. Stephen admired his headstrong and carefree outlook on life, and soon enough his influence began to have a positive and intoxicating effect.

"You could tell they were good for each other; we were happy Stephen had found someone who could ignite a new confidence in him," said Ronan. "Eloy came at the perfect time for Stephen. It had been so difficult for him up until then and then suddenly you could see something in him spark up. We were totally behind him."

The normally ultra-guarded Stephen began to let his guard down and embrace his new found romance with less paranoia than his previous relationships, which had been kept strictly off radar. He may not have been ready for the wild abandonment of a public love affair, but as his mind became increasingly frazzled by the constant lies and deceits, he had never been in more need of a normal relationship.

But while his new love was blossoming, by his own admission, the wheels of his double life were beginning to fall off rapidly, even to the extent that he found it difficult to relate to his beloved fans. "Sometimes I would get grouchy with them and a fan would say 'Are you OK Stephen?' and I'd be thinking, 'No, there's a problem, but I can't tell you'. For the first few years it wasn't so much of a problem, but in the last few, when we got bigger and bigger with more attention, it got harder."

With Eloy's arrival on the scene Stephen couldn't keep his excitement and exhilaration at finding a true love to himself. One evening, following one of their sell-out concerts, his bandmate Keith Duffy asked him if there was anyone special in his life. "He's six-foot-three, brown eyes, brown hair, 26 and very kind," he enthused with an honesty and clarity he had struggled to display with any of his previous romances. Keith knew immediately that Stephen had turned a corner.

Within days Eloy was introduced to Stephen's bandmates, and it didn't take him long to become part of the Boyzone family. During the band's seemingly never-ending tour and promotion dates, Eloy would ride along with the wives and girlfriends, hanging out back stage and disappearing off through the throngs of fans to spend evenings in Stephen's luxurious hotel suites. Stephen would finally have someone special he could confide in, share his innermost fears with, and even begin to think about a future together.

When the band left the stage each night around 11 p.m., Keith, Ronan, Mikey and Shane would invariably congregate in the bar of whatever hotel they were staying in and get stuck into a few beers to help them come down from the adrenaline rush of their latest sell-out show.

Stephen would rarely make an appearance with his bandmates. Instead he would be relaxing in his suite with Eloy, watching movies, eating late night snacks from the room service menu and living the closest thing that Stephen had experienced to a "normal life". They would talk about Stephen's upbringing. He would confide about his, at times, strained relationship with his parents and his fears about being outed. Eloy was a good listener and he would also offer advice and experience from his own trials and tribulations as a gay man trying to cut it in the pop business.

While Eloy's arrival on the scene was welcomed by the rest of the band, Stephen was still gripped by the fear that if word got out about his falling for the Dutch singer it could destroy everything the band had achieved.

"The pressure on me was immense even though I was so happy to have found Eloy," Stephen told me just two years ago. "Looking back I remember feeling very strongly that it wasn't just about my reputation or what secrets I was keeping from the fans – it was about the whole band. If there had been a backlash against me over the Eloy relationship then it could have brought the whole group down. If you had asked me right then what I thought would have happened if my relationship became public knowledge, I would have probably said 'It's going to be the end of the band.'"

With such fears weighing heavily on Stephen's mind, he and Eloy conducted their romance with the discretion and caution of an FBI operation. Every meticulous detail would be carefully planned to perfection so that the risk factor was reduced to virtually zero.

At the time of boy band mania it wouldn't be unheard of for tabloid newspapers to plant reporters for nights on end in the groups' hotels on the off chance they'd land a bumper sex scandal story, clocking a singer escaping to their room with a groupie, or better still, a famous admirer.

Stephen had been on the road too long with Boyzone to fall for such stings. Every effort would be made to keep their love affair strictly off limits to the public, with only a select few ever knowing the true secret of what was going on.

Fearing they could be snapped by a photographer in public after concerts or public appearances, Stephen would climb into one car and Eloy another as they trekked back to the same hotel, arriving an hour apart. They would also go to incredible lengths to check in at different times, therefore lessening the chances of an eagle-eyed receptionist or doorman clocking their movements and linking the couple.

Money was no obstacle for Gately, who by now was pocketing around £500,000 for every tour, so he thought nothing of booking the two rooms, under pseudonyms, knowing that they would only ever use one bed. When Stephen reached the room he would call Eloy on his mobile and tell him the number.

"It was all very cloak and dagger," said Stephen. "But we knew we couldn't take any chances. We accepted that we had a relationship that would be conducted behind closed doors. Eloy had been in a band too and he knew the risks and the sacrifices you had to make so we were happy to just be in love and having to keep it secret was just something we accepted and got on with. We used to be under so much pressure to hide our love for each other. We arrived an hour apart in different cars. Then we would meet up when we were sure no one would notice. Looking back on it, I don't know how we didn't go mad."

On one short holiday break that they planned together Eloy and Stephen even booked on different flights to reach the destination, fearing any reservation under both their names would trigger alarm bells. "I remember it being so difficult to let our guard down because we were not yet openly gay," said Eloy. "Ronan used to help us keep things quiet. We had to be clever about the way we hid our relationship."

While they may have accepted that it was a price worth paying, their paranoia was misplaced. For little could they have imagined that their six-month affair would be compromised not by a prying journalist or indiscreet hotel employee - but by a man employed to work at the heart of the band.

During every Boyzone tour, even to this date, the group works with a close-knit team of security guards, who are entrusted into the band's closest quarters. They are privy to the intricate details of all the singers' lives, and as such are regarded as the most trustworthy employees.

It was during the Boyzone tour of 1999 that one of their minders began paying close and unwelcome attention to Eloy. Over the long nights of sell out concerts he would chat to the Dutchman as Stephen poured out his heart and soul on stage. Eloy felt he had nothing to fear since the same individual was often an instrumental part of their strategy to spend time together.

After the gigs the minder would be asked to shepherd Stephen and Eloy away, albeit in different cars, but always with instructions to tell the driver to take them to the same place. As a regular pattern began to emerge, the man began to make a stream of notes charting dates, times, movements and even hotel locations where he had enabled the stars to spend time together. All the while he would continue under the guise of being a loyal employee of the band. As Stephen and Eloy blissfully settled into a routine, their security guard was plotting to expose them to the highest bidding tabloid, certain that he would attract a bumper pay day for leaking the biggest showbiz shocker for years.

One afternoon in June 1999 he called up the news desk of *The Sun* newspaper. "I have a story you might be interested in," he said, trying to compose himself. "It's about Stephen Gately. You know, the Boyzone singer. To be honest I've never done anything like this before but...well I've been working on their tour and he's been dating a Dutch pop singer...and I, well, I want to sell the story."

Any doubts that the newspaper would have had over the betrayal were soon allayed when he went to the newspaper offices, under the guarantee of anonymity, to hand over a detailed dossier of the couple's activities over the previous three months. It was all there in colourful detail. The dates, the times, what they were wearing, where they were staying. As the newspaper's top journalists examined the documents carefully for ten minutes the security guard was asked if he would sign a sworn affidavit, confirming that Stephen and the Dutch singer had been in a relationship. A provisional fee was agreed and he readily signed the contract, handing over the brown file to seal Gately's fate.

The following morning Gately was, as usual, in a hotel room with Eloy. The evening before they had enjoyed a romantic dinner for two in his luxury suite, scoffing on their favourite meal of steak and French fries and enjoying a glass of expensive wine. Suddenly Stephen's mobile phone rang. He walked across the room in his fluffy white dressing gown and unplugged it from the wall socket where it had been charging.

"Stephen, we have a bit of a problem", announced the familiar voice of the band's PR, who had been hired by the group to take care of all their media requests, interviews and promotions. "I think we need to talk. It's about you and Eloy - someone is selling the story to *The Sun*."

Stephen's heart sunk to the pit of his stomach. He momentarily covered the phone and tried desperately to regain his composure. Sitting down on the end of the bed his hand began shaking violently as the colour drained from his ashen face. He turned to Eloy and slowly shook his head. Eloy placed his hand on Stephen's left shoulder but he was inconsolable. Seven years after joining Boyzone, the game was up.

CHAPTER FIVE

Out of the Darkness, Into the Fire

Stephen Gately must have felt he was living a charmed life by the time June 1999 came around. He was entering his sixth year in the biggest pop band on the planet and as the number one hits rolled in, so did the adulation and money. By striking up a romance with Eloy his world finally seemed complete. He discovered for the first time the inner joy of having contentment in both his professional and personal life.

But the honeymoon period was short-lived. Just as Stephen was enjoying the excitement of his first serious long-term romance, he was faced with the ultimate dilemma when The Sun contacted him to announce they had discovered his most closely guarded secret. The star had been sold out by the opportunistic minder, who had approached the newspaper with an offer to tell-all about Stephen's secret gay relationship, in return for a big payday.

As Stephen contemplated the carnage about to be unleashed on his career in the press, he hung the "Do not disturb" sign over his Dublin hotel room door and turned off his mobile phone. First he cried, then his fear turned to frustration and anger as he raged to Eloy: "Why won't they just let me be? What have I ever done to deserve this?"

For the next thirty minutes the couple weighed up the options.

Stephen's press officer had warned him that the newspaper was ready to run with the story and there was not a minute to be wasted. The choice was simple; to allow the story to run in all its salacious glory, emblazoned across the front pages like a shameful expose, or to take the only other option, tell all himself, which would have seemed unfathomable just hours before. Stephen was offered a chance to confess all to the newspaper and admit the shocking revelation that would rock the showbiz world and Boyzone's army of fans.

Eloy put his arm around Stephen reassuringly: "If you do it your way then at least you can have some pride," he reasoned. "Otherwise this bastard gets to make thousands out of trying to destroy you. Please, Stephen, be brave and admit what is happening." Stephen thought about it for the minute, and then turned his phone back on. He called Caroline, his PR girl, his voice a soft quiver of nerves. "It's me. I've spoken to Eloy and I....well I'm ready to say I'm gay. Let's do it."

Within minutes the news was scrambled from Boyzone's marketing department to *The Sun* editor's office. An agreement was hatched that two of their reporters – Rav Singh and Sam Carlisle – would take the first flight from London to Dublin, where Boyzone were performing a gig that evening.

As Stephen arrived at the venue on the north bank gate of the River Liffey three hours before the concert, he looked nervously out over the gates where over 200 fans had already gathered, as they did before every one of their shows. He asked himself if those beaming, adoring expressions on their faces would turn to anger when they discovered the secret he had kept from them. Time would soon tell.

But Stephen had little time to dwell. He pulled down his baseball cap, took a deep breath and lowered his head to duck under the door frame leading to the band's backstage compound. Waiting in a cramped dressing room at the back of the hospitality area were the two reporters, armed with a list of questions and tape recorders. There was no going back now.

Before he started, Stephen asked Louis Walsh, who had been instrumental in setting up the delicate interview, to summon Eloy. Right on cue the tall Dutchman emerged from the corridor, a reassuring and familiar face, to support the singer as he made his brave confession.

"He wanted to walk down the street holding the hand of his then boyfriend, Eloy de Jong, without fear. He wanted the same freedoms his bandmates enjoyed with their girlfriends," said Carlisle of that meeting. "Eloy sat beside him, Stephen told me and my colleague Rav Singh that he was in love. He told me 'at school I dated girls but by the time I was 15 I knew they weren't for me'. He praised his bandmates for their unreserved friendship and support. Two hours later I watched Ronan Keating and the rest of the group perform brilliantly to their home crowd of 9,000 hysterical girls."

That night Gately gave everything he had to the performance. "He feared it would be his last gig and that everyone would turn on him after it," revealed Louis. "I think he just gave it everything that night knowing what was going to hit the headlines the next day. Even when faced with that stress Stephen was a total professional. Nobody would have known what he was going through on stage that night."

Later that evening, Stephen and Eloy, knowing there was little point keeping up the guise that they were just friends, finally left a Boyzone concert together for the first time. No separate cars, no decoys, no pseudonyms at the hotels and no separate rooms. Stephen should have been feeling terrified. He had been dreading this moment ever since he joined Boyzone; the moment where they would discover the real man behind the whiter than white pop facade. But all he could feel was exhilaration. The burden of years of lies, excuses, fronts and deception were about to be lifted. And whether Stephen liked it or not, there was no going back.

The Sun had agreed not to print the story until Stephen had time to speak to his family. He knew that it was one thing unleashing the beast on himself as he jetted around the world, but the impact for his family, who still lived around the Sheriff Street area, would be cataclysmic.

The following day Stephen and Eloy flew to Milan for the next leg of the Boyzone tour. That night, as they ordered room service, there was an eerie, unnerving calm. No phones ringing, no photographers chasing after them, no news reporters hiding undercover to catch them out. Then, in one earth shattering second, all that changed forever.

As the dramatic 11 o'clock news theme tune struck up on Sky, Gately's confession was there for the world to see – in full explosive detail. "Tonight on *Sky News*," announced the presenter "Boyzone's Stephen Gately reveals 'I'm gay.'"A giant shot of *The Sun's* front page filled the screen, along with a picture of the singer, proclaiming: *Boyzone Stephen: I'm gay and I'm in love.*

"We were sitting watching Sky News," Stephen recalled in 2001, "And we were saying 'Oh God, that story's coming out tomorrow! Wonder how big it's going to be? And they said 'Here's the headlines' and it comes up. My jaw dropped. All the tragedies in the world – the famines, the earthquakes, people dying – and the three biggest tabloids chose to put me on the cover. We were in the *New York Times*. Little Stephen from Sheriff Street, Dublin, you know. In the *New York Times!*"

In the carefully orchestrated interview Stephen gave his reasons for coming out, with not a mention of the behind-the-scenes drama which really prompted his moment of confession. "I only hope they understand how important it is for me to reveal I'm gay," he said. "I think the moment is now right to tell the world who I really am. Boyzone have just finished a sell-out UK tour and we've sold millions of records, but I can't begin to enjoy that success until I can be the real me."

As Stephen's every word was absorbed by stunned, heartbroken, supportive and shocked fans alike, the public reaction was overpoweringly positive. As the star enjoyed a tidal wave of support, he must have wondered why he had taken so long, endured so much heartache and misery and shrouded himself in such agonising secrecy for so long.

"Ten years later, I was invited backstage at Wembley Arena for Boyzone's reunion tour in June. Stephen, still gorgeous, greeted me with a hug, a kiss and a huge smile," remembers Carlisle, the journalist who broke the story. "I asked him - did we do the right thing?"

He said: "Of course. I've never regretted it. That was the most difficult interview I've ever done - but it allowed me to live my life."

But while the overriding wave of support from the fans was carrying Stephen buoyantly into the future, word soon reached the singer that there was a decidedly less than enthusiastic reaction back home on Sheriff Street, not least from his mother, Margaret. Her blunt but honest reaction to Stephen's revelations would have reminded the star that while the worldwide alliance of Boyzone fans may be an understanding bunch, Dublin's north side was a less forgiving place when it came to homosexuality.

"It was always his own business and that's the way it should be," she said pointedly, leaving little room for doubt. "He never wanted people to know. It's not as if he's a paedophile or a murderer."

Alarmingly for Stephen, Margaret appeared acutely conscious of the impact his monumental moment of truth would have on the family in Dublin. "The effect it will have on the whole family will be phenomenal," she warned, fanning the flames. "Everyone has been so worried and anxious about it. The lad's fans are nearly all children - just young girls. I don't know how parents are going to explain this to them. Most are too young to even know what gay is. They will see all this about Stephen and demand to know what it's about."

Margaret could not be criticised for honesty as she reluctantly assessed how Stephen's revelations would impact on matters much closer to home. But they were in stark contrast to Stephen's strategy to pepper the announcement with positive and optimistic messages that would be absorbed by his loyal fans.

Stephen was certainly not enamoured by Margaret's comments: "I want an upbeat message out there," he confided to his bandmates. "I don't want people thinking my own family have turned their backs on me. Of all the people who should be supporting me, it's not the fans or my bandmates, it's my family! I thought I had done my family proud and they owe me back now. I need them on my side, publicly and privately," Stephen mused.

But if Margaret's reaction was less than what Stephen had been hoping for he could bank on a warmer reception from his celebrity friends. Dozens of stars rallied around, led by Elton John who, in typically larger than life style, had a huge bouquet of 100 flowers sent to him as soon as the news hit the front pages. "Graham Norton sent a beautiful letter, Elton sent flowers, George Michael rang and... um...even Billy Connolly said 'Who gives a shit?'" recalled Stephen. "There was no homophobia at all, except the odd slagging from lads on the street, but let them."

The tabloids handled the affair with unusual sympathy, even setting up phone help lines for fans. Apparently there were more calls than when Take That split up. The teen press was also unswervingly positive. *Smash Hits* put him on the cover, the first time the best selling magazine had done so with an openly gay man. Editor at the time Joe McKie said: "Times had changed. It was the first time a 'sitting' teen idol had ever come out. I'm not sure we could have done it 15 years before, but the kids were overwhelmingly supportive. It actually brought them closer to him. It brought out their maternal instinct."

For Louis Walsh, the man who had helped created the myth of a girl-hungry heterosexual boy band hunk, Stephen's public revelations were an uncomfortable step into the unknown. Louis had as much to lose as the singer himself, after working tirelessly around the clock for seven years to transform them into the world-conquering sensation they now were.

Before Boyzone, Louis had enjoyed plenty of success in Ireland. But his young boy band starlets were his passport to the big time both in terms of money and reputation. "I was worried about what the fans would think, I really was," Louis confesses, looking back at the turbulent time. "I mean we were going into uncharted waters and none of us knew exactly what would happen.

"There was a lot of fear that the backlash could be so intense that it would end the group. Of course that was something that worried us greatly because we had all given our lives, hearts and even our souls to Boyzone. For every penny that was made and for every hit that topped the charts, there had been so many sacrifices. But in all honesty the first concern was that Stephen would be OK. That's what was most important.

"We sat in a room as a band, and Shane Lynch just turned around and said: 'Look everyone, if this ends the group then so be it. It's more important that Stephen is happy.' After he said that it put everything into perspective. I think we all just kind of shrugged our shoulders, gave him a hug and got on with the business of the band."

***

At last Stephen was free from the demons that had blighted his rise to stardom and he wasn't going to stop with the big announcement. During a weekend break with his boyfriend the pair began discussing their plans for the future.

The boys were taking a six month break after completing their tour and, for the first time since they met, Stephen and Eloy would be able to live a normal life.

"Move to Holland with me," suggested Eloy, out of the blue. "It's a place where we can be totally ourselves. We won't have the press running around after us. We won't have to watch our backs every second. We can just enjoy what we have."

For Stephen, who just ten years before was living a modest existence on Dublin's Northside, Eloy's big idea might have sounded whimsical at best. But to the Dutchman's surprise, Stephen turned to him immediately and broke into a beaming smile, saying "Yes, yes. Let's do it. When can we go?"

Until then the couple had split their time between Stephen's secluded five-bedroom home in Wicklow and his apartment in London. But they convinced themselves that this move to Holland would be their real home - a place away from the prying eyes of the public where they could lay the foundations for a serious long-term relationship.

For the first few months the couple enjoyed the inevitable honeymoon period. Stephen co-invested with Eloy in a £1.25 million, three bedroom riverfront house on the outskirts of Amsterdam. They bought a Shih Tzu called Joey, a Cocker Spaniel named Woody, and Casper the Persian cat.

"We have a park just round the corner where we walk the dogs and feed the swans, and that's breathtaking," Stephen would say enthusiastically of his new-found haven. "And our land is on water, anyway. We have a boat so we go off down the canals with the dogs and a picnic on sunny days and read our books.

"I love being cosy and at home with Eloy. I always have to have incense, and sometimes I light 40 candles a night. We used to be addicted to Jo Malone. She does these scented candles, and the smell!"

Towards the end of that summer Stephen could justifiably rejoice. He had even managed to find the time to pen some songs about his experience of coming out in front of the whole world. "I've come up with these really strong, meaningful lyrics," he told Eloy. "Maybe one day I'll get to put them on a proper record."

***

Behind the scenes, however, something was brewing that would bring him crashing down to earth in dramatic style. Gately may have had two loves in his life at the time – Boyzone and Eloy – but he would discover as the band enjoyed their summer hiatus that Louis Walsh and the band's lead singer Ronan Keating were locked in secret talks that would lead to a Boyzone bombshell.

Ronan wanted to go solo and Louis, with his increasing catalogue of industry knowledge and contacts, could make it happen in spectacular style.

Little did Stephen know that when the band returned to work in September to record the group's new single, *Every Day I Love You,* the clock was rapidly ticking on the band's future.

It had all seemed so positive when they congregated in the studio that day. Stephen and his bandmates had been summoned to a meeting in London to plot the next six months. "We're releasing a single in December and we can easily sell out 40 dates over Christmas and the New Year," announced Louis in typically forthright style. "It's going to be busy, busy, busy."

Ronan was equally buoyant, cracking the old familiar jokes with his bandmates that they had ribbed each other with during six years on the road together. They even vowed to make their next tour, due to kick off just before Christmas, their wildest ever: "Steo may even get in a round of drinks this time round," joked Ronan. "Let's make this one to remember."

When tickets went on sale the post Gately coming out response was as frenzied as before. It was clear Boyzone's enthusiastic army of diehards had accepted his declared sexuality without question – and were as happy as ever to stump up their hard-earned £35 for a concert ticket.

Every show, spanning London, Manchester, Belfast, Glasgow, Cardiff and the last hurrah at the Point in Dublin sold out at lightening speed. "The truth is, Stephen coming out actually increased our ticket and album sales," Shane Lynch said at the time. "We won over a lot of gay fans to add to the female fanatics. It was a win-win."

For Stephen it was the ultimate validation of his actions, not to mention the guarantee of a timely pay day, as he continued to maintain mortgages on properties in Wicklow, London and now Amsterdam. Along with Mikey, Keith, Ronan and Shane, Stephen signed on the dotted line for the concerts and looked forward to hitting the stage again.

But he soon sensed that all was not well. His bandmates were arguing, Ronan seemed distant, and Shane appeared to be on a self-destruct mission, capped by a shambolic appearance at the MTV Europe Music Awards where he drunkenly took to the stage in a shabby tracksuit and launched into a four-letter tirade: "There has been a lot of fucking shit in the newspapers about us splitting up. We're not going anywhere," he fumed. Behind him Stephen's face said it all as his smile turned to a scornful grimace.

There was war when they got off stage. "What the hell are you doing?" screamed the band's press officer. "How the fuck are we going to explain this one. Jesus, we're meant to be Boyzone - the clean-cut good guys." Shane nonchalantly shrugged his shoulders and continued twirling a white toothpick in his mouth.

Stephen handled matters in his own more measured way, pulling Shane to the side in a backroom at The Point in Dublin and asking: "Are you OK? Is there something you need to talk about? This isn't good Shane, this isn't good at all."

But while the rest of the band were dealing with the fallout from Shane's angry rant there was something more disturbing on Stephen's agenda. For the first time since he and Ronan had teamed up as the wing men that carried Boyzone for all those years, he was beginning to question his bandmate's true intentions.

Ronan had already enjoyed a summer break that saw him top the charts with his first solo single, the *Notting Hill* movie soundtrack *When You Say Nothing At All*. He had become an outright star on his own, commanding red carpets at premieres and being photographed with celebrity pals wherever he travelled.

Between hanging out with Julia Roberts and Hugh Grant, he even began openly talking about his desire to release a solo album when the group's next tour ended, although he insisted: "It won't affect the band at all. We are all going to do our own things for a year and then get back together."

Stephen suspected that Ronan's foray into the individual limelight may have given him a taste for more on a permanent basis, and he wasn't wrong. His suspicions were raised when he noticed Ronan becoming evasive when he broached the subject of future plans.

As Christmas approached, and with the group due to complete their latest tour at The Point in January, Stephen began chatting to the rest of the band about their next album. "Everyone was thinking album, songs, singles and things like that. But Ronan was, well, he was just very vague about the whole thing," Stephen told me. "Sure, we were all going off to try out our own things for a while. But looking back, obviously all the plans were being laid down for his solo work as a permanent rather than temporary move. And I remember thinking that it was odd that he wouldn't talk about anything beyond the next month because he was always really into mapping things out and planning everything to perfection. I kind of tiptoed around the whole thing and never got a straight answer. But looking back now I think I knew in my heart that, as a band, we were in trouble."

Stephen, as he often did at times of crisis, turned to Eloy for guidance. "You are a singer as much as him," his boyfriend assured him. "If Ronan is going to go solo for a while then you can do the same thing. It's not just all about him."

Boosted by Eloy's rallying call, Stephen began to call friends in the music business and lay down the foundations for a post-Boyzone career of his own. "Don't tell anyone about this yet," he would urge those he confided in. "I can't be seen to be making plans until I find out what's going on with Ronan. But I think I'd like to release something in the summer."

But first there was the not insignificant task of the band's final show of the tour, to be filmed for a special DVD that would net each member of the group another £200,000. Stephen dutifully masked his suspicions about Ronan as they took to the stage that night for one last time in Dublin.

Ronan delivered an A1 acting job by announcing to a live TV audience who had tuned in on Sky that: "We're not going anywhere. We'll see you again soon." The boys linked arms and waved gleefully to their fans, who could have never imagined, given their united front, that this was the last time that Boyzone would set foot on stage again together for more than seven years.

***

For Stephen, the break-up would bring with it a crushing reality that would see his life descend into free fall and heartache.

Just days after the finale concert in Dublin the press was rife with rumours that Ronan was planning a permanent getaway from the group. Stephen distracted himself by following through on those calls he had made to his music industry pals.

Now the picture was becoming clear in his mind. If Ronan couldn't guarantee the band a future of their own, then Stephen would take care of matters himself and release his own solo album. He managed to secure a one-album deal with Polydor, who vowed to put their considerable weight behind his bid to give Ronan a run for his money.

Stephen hurried to the studio and laid down the lyrics for what would be his debut single – New Beginning. It was a bold and, some would say, overzealous statement of his sexual liberation. The hugely produced track was accompanied by a multi-dimensional video where an angelic Gately sang amid a backdrop of water falls and nature.

"It's the most over-produced garbage I've seen in a long time," moaned legendary producer Pete Waterman, seemingly unimpressed with the singer's big budget production.

Fans however, rallied behind his solo effort, albeit not with the same devotion as they had with Boyzone. Still, they lapped it up in sufficient numbers to take it to the UK charts number three slot, which Stephen insisted was "great news. I would have been happy with anything in the top ten."

Charting high also gave Stephen a passport to the coveted BBC *Top Of The Pops* show, where he smiled triumphantly on stage in a white jacket and performed with the impressive back-up of gospel singers, violinists and a full five-piece band.

Stephen was buoyant. He had successfully negotiated a career minefield over the previous twelve months; coming out, going solo and now putting his lyrics and music at the mercy of the critics and unforgiving public. Yet somehow, things could not have worked out better. He felt blessed.

It was during this period that I would meet his boyfriend Eloy for the first and only time. Stephen invited me to meet him in the penthouse suite in Bono's Clarence Hotel, as he continued to frantically promote his album at every opportunity. He had learnt from his mentor Louis Walsh that you could never do too many interviews or talk to enough fans, because every one of them represented a chance to sell another record.

That afternoon it struck me how Stephen appeared more confident and assured in himself than ever. He looked the picture of health and happiness as he sipped a sparkling water and munched on a chicken sandwich. He told me how Eloy had brought true balance to his life. Exuding the joys of his personal and professional happiness he revealed: "We spend every possible minute together when we are not working. We've come through an amazingly hard time, but have survived against all the odds."

As he spoke to me Eloy burst through the door, having just returned from a city centre shopping spree with a surprise present for Stephen. He couldn't hide his delight; "That's the kind of thing he does all the time. But I'm not opening it now because it could be something naughty."

He told me how they had settled together and were enjoying a normal life. "We watch a movie, have a barbecue with friends or relax in the garden with a bottle of wine." Then he leapt to his feet in a frenzy of energy and excitement, grabbing a CD and slamming it into the high tech music system across the room. "Do you want to hear one of the songs from the album? This is *Judgement Day*. I wrote it about the day before the story about me being gay was about to break. It's similar for someone who is waiting on death row in a way. There's a total fear of the unknown, a real helplessness.

"I remember sitting in my hotel the night before and it was absolutely terrifying. Most gay people experience the anxiety of having to come out to their families. But there I was waiting to come out to the whole world. There's nothing that can describe that feeling."

***

Sadly, over the next few months, while Stephen was happy to wax lyrical about his new-found contentment, the cracks were beginning to appear as the dynamics of their relationship changed.

Until Stephen had come out the pair were united with an "us against the world" mentality, carefully guarding their secret relationship and knowing that the stakes were perilously high. They could live a liberated and exciting, on-the-edge existence behind closed doors, because a "normal" lifestyle would have been impossible. After Stephen's announcement that all changed. They had the validation they desperately craved, but with it they also had all the responsibility and accountability that goes with a conventional relationship.

"Real life started getting in the way of the private world we had built up to protect ourselves," said Stephen during an interview he gave me last year. "You walk around in a little bubble for a while and nobody can hurt you. When you have such a big secret, it kind of empowers you in a funny kind of way. You get the siege mentality where you are battling against everyone else. When everything was out there in the open it was an incredible, liberating feeling. So you run off and set up home and start doing normal things for the first time and that is just heaven. Then you walk around in a buzz for a few months just getting off on the normality of it all. Normality is such a foreign thing when you have been living in the closet, where you spent endless nights dreaming about what it would be like to have a proper boyfriend and enjoy the simple things in life together."

While the public recognition they so desperately craved was assured, soon enough the simple things weren't enough to bind Stephen and Eloy together with the same unconditional bond they had enjoyed for the previous 18 months. The romantic gestures, constant travelling, and the public and private pledges of their undying love were all slowly ebbing away under the pressure of Stephen's solo career.

Adding to the couple's private pressures were Stephen's poor album sales. When his album New Beginning hit record stores in July of 2000, the singer was praying for a top five hit. He knew in the modern day environment of disposable stars and short-term deals that anything less would put him and his credibility under serious pressure.

When the album performed less than spectacularly and peaked at number nine in the UK charts, Stephen was privately devastated.

What made it worse was that when his bandmate Ronan released his self-titled debut solo album just a month later, he rocketed straight to the number one spot. Stephen feared his career was petering out while Ronan's was being greeted with the fanfare, pomp and ceremony of a solo pop star. Behind the scenes Stephen must have felt that Ronan was stealing his thunder as the two went head to head, just weeks apart, in a battle to show there was life beyond the confines of Boyzone. By the time his follow up single, I Believe, peaked at a lowly number 11, Stephen was really beginning to feel the heat.

A solo stint that had begun with the powerful optimism of a man freed from the chains of his past was now bringing him down. As rumours swept the music industry that he would soon be dropped by his label, Stephen desperately threw himself into a non-stop schedule of promotion and performance over the whole of Christmas and well into the New Year. This time, instead of being joined everywhere by the normally inseparable Eloy, Stephen was going it alone during most of his travels.

"I was in a zone where it was all about work, promotion, doing gigs. It wasn't right," Stephen later accepted. "I shouldn't have pushed Eloy away. I wasn't there for him." As Stephen ran up the air miles trying to save his career, Eloy, back in Holland, was becoming increasingly impatient and irritated.

Just a year earlier Stephen had been enthusiastically plotting the next Boyzone album, considering a solo career and extolling the virtues of his love life. Now he was faced with the tormenting prospect of losing all three. It would prove to be a cross that was almost too much to bear.

CHAPTER SIX
Darkest Days

Stephen held the phone tight to his ear. He knew from the disheartened tone at the other end of the line that it wasn't good. His heart sunk and his pulse raced as he plucked up the courage to ask the question but, deep down, he already knew the answer.

"Is everything OK? Is there a problem?"

The Polydor representative paused briefly: "It's like this Stephen. We think you are extremely talented and you've been fantastic to us. But we're going to have to let you go."

Stephen sat down, his stomach tied up in knots and his emotions swirling with a dizzying effect. Nerves, embarrassment, disappointment, anger, despair. How would he face his fans with the news? What was he going to say to Eloy? What would the other Boyzone lads think? How would the press treat his spectacular fall from grace?

To Stephen his music career was everything. His whole life had been devoted to hitting the big time, proving wrong those cynical doubters who poked fun at his relentless ambition while stuck on Sheriff Street.

Now, in June 2001, he was facing the ultimate humiliation –

getting the axe from his own record company. In Stephen's heart he knew the clouds had been gathering for awhile. Only one of his three singles had made the top ten, and the last two had petered out with barely a whimper.

The bombast and hype around his opening single had quickly subsided. The loyal Boyzone fans that had rallied to buy up multiple copies of New Beginning were now aligning themselves with Ronan, who was enjoying adulation and success on a massive scale with hits like *Life Is a Roller Coaster* and *Lovin' Each Day*.

No matter what happened, Stephen had always reassured himself that at least the Boyzone fans would stand by him. "There is an army of them out there," he would say. "They are backing Ronan but they're bound to get behind me too. If I can find some kind of a sound that bridges what I want to do and what Boyzone were achieving then I could be on to something." But as the sales figures tumbled it seemed that even the die-hards had deserted him.

If Stephen was honest with himself, he knew his heart had not been in the project since it became clear that his star was on the wane. "My soul wasn't in it," he later confessed. "I just didn't want to do it. I didn't want to talk about the latest record, appear on TV or do radio promotions. I hated it after a while."

In truth, Stephen had been entirely enthusiastic about his solo stint at the beginning, when he wholeheartedly believed he could conquer the charts all over again as a solo star. But when his final single, Stay, peaked at number 13 in the UK charts that May it was clear to the bank rolling executives in Polydor that Gately was far from the cash cow they could bank on when he was part of the

Boyzone machine. With ruthless and unforgiving profit margins and a desire for instant commercial success, they reasoned that Stephen had been given ample opportunity to make the transition from boy band star to solo success. As far as they were concerned they weren't running a charity for former boy band has-beens, and their loyalty only ran so deep – and even that turned out to be pretty shallow.

As the executives at Polydor's London office gathered to seal Stephen's fate, they looked at his band mate Ronan Keating, who had been storming the charts with four top six singles – including two number ones – and the math was simple. Stephen was not a profitable proposition. He was a liability and a luxury they simply couldn't afford.

"The facts speak for themselves," said one of their high ranking music experts, with a handful of music industry spread sheets and graphs at hand. "Stephen isn't selling enough records to break even, let alone make us money. We've given him good backing but it's simply not working. I'm not sure he even wants it that badly – he's turned down half a dozen interview requests in the last week alone." And so the decision was signed off by their highest ranking board members and Stephen would be "let go" - the industry's euphemism for firing one of their own stars.

Stephen thanked the caller for his time and hung up, then buried his head in his hands and began to sob.

It was a bitter blow but one he had brought on himself. His relationship with Eloy had already been placed under huge strain from his relentless work schedule. But what had it all been for? Now he was faced with a fractured career and a precariously balanced relationship.

He gathered his composure and joined Eloy in the other room: "It's over," he said, still wiping tears from his eyes. "They've dropped me. I can't believe it, but they've fucking dropped me."

Eloy put his arms around Stephen, trying to convince him everything would work out, but he was inconsolable. He felt cheated and bitter as he remembered how just a year-and-a-half before everything had been so different.

He thought back to how he had stood on stage in Dublin with his Boyzone bandmates as Ronan, so long his close friend and confidante, announced misleadingly to fans "We'll be back soon". But now, faced with his own failures, the heartbreaking reality of life as a defunct pop singer had truly set in.

"I didn't even realise the day we split up that it was over," he sobbed, surveying the career carnage that lay before him. "I just thought we were having a break. Now there is nothing. It's over."

Over the coming weeks the couple hid away in their waterside home on the outskirts of Amsterdam as Stephen battled to come to terms with the blunt realities of his fading career. But as the reality of his fallen career became glaringly clear, the walls of self-doubt and despair were rapidly closing in and Stephen knew he had to get away. He told Eloy he was leaving for London to try to salvage at least something. Maybe he could land a TV role, something in the acting game or, better still, convince his Boyzone band mates to get back together. It was all wishful thinking.

Stephen's desperate plan triggered yet another argument with his lover: "What about us? I have hardly seen you for the past six months and now you want to go back to London," Eloy was incandescent with rage, punching his fist against the wall in pure frustration. "It's as if I'm not enough for you. It's career, career, career. What about love? What about life?"

But Eloy's protestations fell on deaf ears. Stephen made a desperate dash back to London, leaving his partner to dwell on their troubles. He hurriedly set up meetings with record executives and producers, TV bosses and talent agencies, but one by one they turned him down.

Anxiety now overwhelmed him. He was still in his twenties, but felt more like an old man well past his sell-by date. The once confident, charismatic young man who lit up on stage with Boyzone at their spectacular live shows was now suffering from a demoralising and debilitating confidence crisis.

"I ended up wondering what the hell am I going to do with my life?" he told me later. "You are in your twenties and you're meant to be starting out this big adventure in life. Yet there was me feeling like I was about to retire. It messes with your mind, something like that. I ended up longing for the life I once had and the future looked so bleak. I was scared out of my mind that I was going to end up old, fat, lonely and without purpose. So I kept calling people and looking for avenues to try to salvage something but suddenly the calls weren't returned anymore and nobody was interested."

Back in Amsterdam Eloy was becoming impatient. He called Stephen: "Look, I think we need to talk," he said impatiently. "Things aren't the same between us. We used to do everything together and now there is this huge gulf between us. I need to know what the hell is going on. I can't live like this."

"What do you want me to do, Eloy?" Stephen snapped. "You knew what you were getting into when you were with me. I'm a singer; I can't be in one place all the time. I love you but you have to let me work too. I need to think of myself right now. I can't just give up."

But for Eloy the damage was done. "Look," he said, pausing briefly. "I think...I think we need to take a break."

Stephen, enraged at Eloy's suggestion, hung up. Minutes later he sent him a text: "I just need your support here. This isn't easy for me either." But there was no reply.

The singer should have been desperately trying to salvage the relationship that only a year before he had publicly proclaimed "the greatest thing I have ever experienced". But he had no fight left. The desperate attempts to save his career, the long, lonely nights away from Eloy and the heartache of life beyond Boyzone had all taken their toll. Stephen felt numb and had nothing more to give.

Still, Stephen tried to plug on with the fading relationship, but his heart was barely in it. Stephen would later blame himself for their split, admitting: "I was too caught up in my work and I wasn't there for Eloy. It wasn't right how I behaved and one day I hope I can make amends."

Suddenly Stephen was more alone than ever. Throughout any

heartache he had endured over his sexuality, the bitter pill of a Boyzone break up and the crippling disappointment of losing his solo contract, the singer had always at least had someone to pick him up when he was down. But now, as far as Stephen could see, there was nobody. His band mates were off pursuing their own goals and Eloy, the love of his life, couldn't even offer him the solace and safety he so desperately needed.

What a difference it was from the heady days of Boyzone. There was never the chance to feel lonely when life was a kaleidoscope of flights, live concerts, adoring fans and TV appearances. His mobile phone, which would once have been buzzing endlessly with calls and text messages about big work projects, exciting new assignments and promotional agendas, was now silent.

Stephen began to spend more time in London while Eloy would hold the fort back in Amsterdam. Every couple of weeks they would reunite, either in London or Amsterdam, and try to keep things going between them for a while longer. In Stephen's mind, the more time he spent in the UK, the better the chance there was of resurrecting his career. But this would turn into a frustrating routine.

As the monotony of everyday life set in, Stephen would attempt to break up the day by taking strolls to his local news agent to buy the papers. Every now and again a young fan would spot him under the peak of his baseball cap. "Hey Stephen, I'm a big fan," they would invariably announce, always followed by the predictable "So when are Boyzone getting back together?"

Stephen would grimace and nod dutifully back, rarely pausing to make conversation. He felt he could no longer relate to those very

Boyzone fans who had given him a life of privilege and success. The heady days of autograph signings and screaming fans seemed like a distant reality.

Soon enough even the strolls to the local shops ended. Stephen would spend hours sitting in his living room watching mind-numbing daytime TV, the monotony only broken when the telephone would ring from a concerned member of his family in Dublin, who hadn't heard from him for a while.

Even that was soon to change. Stephen was on a downward spiral and seemed intent on cutting himself off from all outsiders. One morning he went as far as throwing his mobile phone away, sending a final text to his friends and family to tell them to reach him on the home phone if ever they needed him.

It was this pattern of increasingly disturbing and withdrawn behaviour that set alarm bells ringing amongst those closest to him. Louis Walsh, among the first to get a concerned call from a friend of Stephen's, feared all was not well. Louis immediately contacted Stephen and begged him to return to Dublin: "You can stay with me," he urged him. "It will be fun. We can get you out for a few nights, have a few beers. It will be good for you."

But Stephen couldn't even enjoy a casual beer anymore after putting an abrupt end to another of his social outlets – drinking. For many it would be a lifestyle-boosting remedy that would enhance both health and happiness. But for Stephen, who was never a big drinker anyway, it was another easy opt-out from social occasions. "If I don't drink then I don't have to go out with the crowd," he would tell himself, instead electing to stay in with Eloy or, when he was on his own, rent a DVD or listen to his old collection of CDs.

Despite Louis' efforts Stephen kept a distance and looked for salvation elsewhere - in the doctor's surgery. In a final desperate bid to overcome his increasingly debilitating moods, and after a showdown with Eloy where the Dutchman had demanded he looked for professional help, he booked in with his doctor: "I've just never felt so low," he explained, pouring out his emotions and fears in the stark and lonely confines of a Harley Street surgery. "I really feel I need something to pick me up. I just can't get over this darkness that has overcome me."

Stephen began taking a course of anti-depressants, telling himself if he just gave them a couple of weeks to kick in he would be back on his feet. Yet still the clouds hung heavy overhead. He convinced himself that he dared not tell his family or friends, for fear they would judge him or, worse still, blame themselves for his fragile state of mind. It would be easier to keep his emotions to himself, he reasoned. In any case, how could he even begin to convince anyone that he was plunged into the depths of despair when he had made millions and lived a heady dream that most would kill for.

Bizarrely, the star found one crutch to hang on to – daily visits to his local gym where he worked out frantically for two hours each session. He would obsessively pace the treadmills, lift weights and push himself to the limit with two hundred sit-ups. Meanwhile, regulars at the upmarket gym would barely get a glance of recognition from the emotionless star. After running to a standstill Stephen would pull on his cap, put his head down and brush past the other gym members engaging in small talk over protein shakes and coffees in the cafe, preferring to return to the seclusion of his lonely flat.

As the months passed Stephen increased his dosage of anti-depressants, hoping that each extra milligram would help ease the pressure and sadness that had engulfed him. But it just made things worse.

To add to his woes, nearly every time he turned on the music channels on his satellite TV, Ronan would pop up, performing at a glamorous awards ceremony, starring in his new video or walking the red carpet with his wife Yvonne at a glitzy London West End premier.

For Stephen it was all too much: "You just feel numb. You just lock out your feelings. It's just really weird. I just wasn't existing," he later said of those bleak days. "I was down in the dumps not knowing where my life was going. And I fell into a huge depression that I couldn't get escape. I was on prescribed drugs for nearly two years but they weren't working. Then I tried all kinds of alternative remedies, herbal prescriptions and other varieties. But they didn't work. I actually gave up drinking alcohol for those two years. But everything I did to try to help myself just seemed to make me more depressed. I couldn't see any way out of it.

"It was my lowest ebb. I was off the drink totally and all my friends and family were trying to persuade me to go out for a beer and have a laugh, go for a night on the town. But I couldn't. I just wanted to stay in. I used to think back to those days when we Boyzone lads had all our parties; we always loved a good drink. But I just couldn't be bothered any more. It was over."

As Stephen's confidence and zest for life visibly dissipated, the once bubbly and energetic singer, who was the brightest face in Boyzone, hit an all time low. He began to think the unthinkable... of ending it all.

"That was the lowest moment for me," Stephen told me in a candid discussion less than a year before he died. "I just started developing these dark thoughts about how bad would it really be if I just ended it. Looking back I was unwell. But the tablets were just making me even lower – I couldn't laugh, I couldn't cry. I had lost myself."

At the time, friends of Gately were privately talking of their fears that he might be suicidal. They rallied around to keep watch on his movements, to make sure he always had someone close at hand he could turn to if he found it all became too much.

A member of Boyzone's entourage who met him by chance at the time said: "I was really shocked when I set eyes on him. He looked vacant and spacey. He said he had given up the drink and was going to the gym five times a week. But he looked like he was out of his tree."

In truth, Stephen was the only one who could help himself. Throughout his entire life he'd battled adversity and overcome huge challenges. More than escaping his humble upbringing in Dublin's north side; more than coming out in front of the world; this would be his biggest challenge. And the stakes were higher than ever.

With no tangible music career and with the loss of his only serious relationship, Stephen may have felt he had little to lose.

But somehow he had to find the strength to drag himself back up from the quagmire of self doubt and depression that he become submerged in.

***

Salvation would come from the most unlikely of sources. Not from the expertise of a top medical professional, or the wisdom of a well-versed psychologist. Instead it arrived in a flurry of feather boas, colour and camp chaos. And it's name was Elton John.

Gately had cut such a forlorn figure during any rare public outings that he was rapidly becoming the talk of showbiz circles. When music industry figures would swap gossip in their private members' clubs in west London, Stephen's name would crop up with alarming frequency. "I've heard he's in a bad way; rumour has it he's in a very dark place," they would speculate as they quaffed champagne in trendy haunts like the Met Bar or the Groucho Club, where tales of showbiz demise were revelled in and even celebrated.

One such tale reached the biggest gay pop star of them all, Elton, as he enjoyed a night out with friends near his holiday villa on the French Riviera. "That's absolutely bloody awful," Elton snapped with a striking emphasis, given he had never met Stephen before. "The poor man. What's his number?" Elton delivered his master plan with the kind of reckless abandon he so famously displayed when organising one of his legendary parties. "Let's get him over for a fucking week here and sort him out."

Minutes later the *Rocket Man* hit maker was patched through to Gately's apartment. Eloy was visiting and on the phone to friends in Amsterdam, so Elton couldn't get through at first, so he left a message on his answer phone: "Stephen darling, it's Elton...You know, Elton John. Anyway sweetie, give me a ring back. I want to get you and Eloy over to France. Call me darling. Bye."

When Stephen played back the message a few minutes later he could barely believe what he was hearing. He could hardly muster a call back from a record company since he had been dropped from his label, and now here was music royalty of the highest order calling him direct at his London apartment. "This has got to be a wind up," he thought, and his suspicions immediately turned to his sister Michelle, with whom he would often trade childish pranks in their ongoing battle to outdo each other.

Still convinced he was falling for an elaborate prank, Stephen called the number. But the extroverted voice at the other end of the line was unmistakable. Elton, in typically impatient style, got straight to the point. "Look Stephen, I've heard you're not in a great way. You've been through a lot my boy and it's a tough business."

Stephen could barely think straight, yet alone find the words to reply. Here was one of the biggest music icons in pop history giving him a pep talk over the phone.

"Listen, there's a few things I think I can help you with...get on the plane to France and I'll see you tonight for a spot of dinner. OK darling?"

Stephen didn't have to think twice. Suddenly the lethargy and resignation that had weighed heavily on his shoulders lifted in a flash. He and Eloy dashed to Heathrow airport and boarded a plane to the south of France, stopping only to wedge a pound coin in a phone box to call Stephen's sister and tell her they was disappearing off with Elton for a few days.

Stephen and Eloy landed two hours later and were quickly whisked by a private driver to a haven of tranquillity and calm. Palm trees towered overhead and the heady scent of orange groves emanated from the hills on a balmy summer evening as they pulled up to the large golden gates of Elton's Cote D 'Azure hideaway. Stephen was already beginning to feel like a changed man, and he hadn't even met the star yet.

Suddenly a huge oak door swung open at the top of a marble walkway, and there, standing triumphantly in his garish yellow-rimmed oversized spectacles, was Elton himself, in all his 5 ft 7 in glory. Stephen broke into a broad smile, like a kid who had waited all year to see Santa Clause. Eloy could barely believe the lavishness of it all. "It's a real pleasure to meet you," Stephen announced with an awkward degree of formality.

But Elton, never one to stand on ceremony, quipped back: "Give us a hug you gorgeous boys," before grabbing Stephen around the waist and leading him inside, leaving his butler to scoop up Stephen's hastily-packed bags. "You've been through a hard time haven't you?" Stephen just nodded with a mixture of embarrassment and anxiety.

As he cautiously followed Elton inside, he could hardly believe his eyes. He had expected the holiday pad to be over the top, but this was hedonism of the highest order. Every corner and turn of the three-story palazzo was dripping in gold, gems and riches. He turned to the left, where marble hallways led to an awe-inspiring garden and pool area, exploding with colour as trailing lobelia and ivy spilled untamed over rustic rock walls that offered sanctuary from the outside world.

Elton sat Stephen down by the pool and called down to his team of cooks to fix them up some dinner. He was in no mood to beat around the bush. "Look Stephen," he said, pausing only to take a sip of his fruit juice cocktail. "I've heard you've been doing a lot of these anti-depressants and things. Take it from me, I'm a reformed drug addict and I've been to the bottom and it is a very, very dark place."

Stephen didn't have to reply. Everything Elton said was striking home. "You need to just ditch the tablets – they work for some people but they're not working for you. You have a bright future ahead of you and you have so much to offer. I have loads of friends in the business who will give you a chance, but first you have to give yourself a chance."

With every sentence Stephen felt the darkness lift. Nothing before had worked; the endless stream of doctors appointments, the anti-depressants, the self imposed booze bans and frantic gym schedules. But this was different. Suddenly he felt understood and valued. There was a reason to live again. There was hope.

Over the coming days Stephen would enjoy a life-changing journey with Elton in the most privileged of surroundings. He wanted for nothing as Elton put his team of butlers, cooks and drivers at his disposal. But the superstar knew from his own experiences that he was going to have to keep Stephen busy if he was to make a real clean break from the tablets that were dictating his moods and lifestyle.

He set up a military style operation, waking Stephen every morning at 8.30 a.m. and bringing him to his private tennis court for a knock about. Stephen, never the sportiest of characters, looked hopelessly out of place with his goofy posture and knobbly knees, barely able to hit the ball back over the net. Next they would return to the villa and Elton would hand Stephen a lighter and ask him to methodically light every candle in the property in anticipation of any guests who were due to drop in for the afternoon. Normally Elton would do the mundane task himself, telling anyone who would listen "I feel like a church chaplain or Mother Teresa." At 1.30 p.m. Elton would have their lunch presented by the pool side, feed the seven dogs affectionately named "The Magnificent Seven", and then they'd have a look around the record stores and antique shops in the village before reading the English papers, which they arrived in the shops around 5pm.

Every now and again Elton would halt everything without any warning and give Stephen an impromptu pep talk. "The most important thing for you to focus on now," he would state with considerable authority, "is the next big thing. You aren't just some singer in Boyzone. Have you thought about doing something on the stage in the West End? It could be the making of you."

Stephen dismissed the idea in his own mind, but was too scared to outwardly contradict Elton. "I'm not sure if I could pull off the whole, you know, acting bit," he said. "I mean I'm not even sure if I want to get back into the business at all. I'm not sure what direction I should take, that's been the problem."

As far as Elton was concerned Stephen was a born star who belonged in the spotlight. It was non-negotiable. "Load of rubbish darling; I have people who can sort all that," Elton promised, before dashing on to their next port of call and changing the subject entirely.

The following night Elton mustered a team of friends and they headed for his favourite restaurant, La Chaumiere in Eze. Stephen was now responding to Elton's irrepressible positivity. Just a week earlier he had been pale and drawn and without purpose. Now here he was, sipping wine under the Riviera moonlight and excitedly plotting the future like a superstar reborn. The world and all its glorious possibilities suddenly felt attainable again. It was as if all his troubles had melted away the moment he drove through Elton's gilded gates.

Leaning slightly forward, Stephen announced: "I've been doing some thinking. When I go home I'm going to audition for a part in a show – they are looking for a new Joseph and I think I can give it a good crack."

Elton put down his knife and fork, turned to Stephen and gave him a huge smacker on the forehead. "My dear boy," he announced regally, at a considerable level of decibels: "You are back! A star is reborn."

CHAPTER SEVEN
Light at the End of the Tunnel

"It's absolutely beautiful," Stephen gasped, his excitement unmistakable. "The colours, the gold threading, I can't believe it," he laughed, inspecting the arms of the weighty coat.

After previews in Oxford and Liverpool in December of 2002, it was now opening night of Stephen's West End stage debut in Andrew Lloyd Webber's *Joseph and the Amazing Technicolor Dreamcoat*, and the singer was backstage in his dressing room. He had become momentarily distracted from his nervousness as he modelled the finished product for the first time. "Worth the wait?" the costume designer smiled. "Worth the wait?" Stephen laughed. "I never even imagined in my wildest dreams that I'd be putting this on," he exclaimed.

They were interrupted by a knock on the door and a member of the floor staff walked in with an enormous bunch of flowers. He placed them beside the lighted stage mirror and passed the singer the small, ivory-coloured card. It was from his trusted friends and mentors and signed *"Love eternally, Elton and David xxx"*

He had come so far because of Elton. He was indebted to him beyond what he could ever repay, but he felt he would give something back by proving himself to them tonight. It was a modest production set, but Stephen would deliver a show-stopping debut performance.

As he sat in his dressing room Stephen wondered what Eloy would make of his latest adventure. Just weeks before their relationship had finally bit the dust and his emotions were still delicate. The couple had grown increasingly polarised from each other since they returned from the life-changing excursion to Elton's home in the South of France.

Stephen, emerging from his battle with depression, was embracing new lifestyle regimes and relaxation techniques. He was immersing himself in practicing yoga, ancient meditation and a complete spiritual overhaul. While Eloy was pleased to see his partner returning to health and happiness, their own shortcomings as a couple were glaringly obvious.

It came to a head one evening as Stephen discussed the amount of time he would have to spend away from their Amsterdam home to concentrate on his role as Joseph: "Look, this is not going to work," Eloy said abruptly. "We may as well take a break; you and I both know it's heading in that direction anyway." They made a pact to remain friends and Stephen packed his bags.

But there was no time for sentiment or regrets tonight. As the heavy, velvet-red curtain went up to *Any Dream Will Do*, he marched on with a chorus of children, literally unable to wipe the smile from his face. The bright lights burned down on him under the heavy coat, but for the first time in years Stephen felt as if he was walking on air. The crowd rose in a rapturous ovation as he finished with a medley of hits from the show, joined onstage by the entire cast.

He was breathless as the audience lights went up to reveal a packed theatre full of excited friends, fans and critics. They were all there to see him and they were enchanted by his acting and singing skills and his engaging stage presence.

The after-party was a huge celebration, but Stephen waited amongst the champagne brigade filled with dread and anticipation for the first reviews from London's sometimes cynical and often demanding theatre critics.

"I'm terrified," he confided in Elton as they waited for the first editions of the papers that would fill the newsstands the following morning. "I don't care how many pats on the back I get tonight. I won't be happy until I see it in black and white. You never know with those fuckers, it can go either way," he stressed.

"Listen to me," insisted Elton. "Andrew believes in you," he reassured, referring to the notoriously hard-to-please Andrew Lloyd-Webber, the mastermind behind the show. "And when the Queen fucking bee says you're talented, who cares about the drones."

Stephen didn't even have time to reply before a stack of newspapers were plonked on a nearby table. The entire production crew gathered round, and the nervous anticipation filled the room. No one knew what was coming.

He felt his heart skip a beat.

"*The Independent,*" a production member announced, pausing for a moment as he scanned the page, "*Gately makes all of the audience fall for him.*"

A round of applause erupted in the crowded room.

He read another review aloud: "*After the numerous re-singings of the songs and several encores you get something which puts the proverbial top hat onto one very colourful coat!*"

Again a triumphant applause rippled through the cast. By the end of the pile Stephen was weak with emotion. "I don't believe it," were the only words he could muster, repeating them over and over as guests, fellow actors and production crew made their way through the crowd to shake his hand.

After all these years he had finally discovered his forte.

It was still a million miles away from the glorious days of playing to thousands of Boyzone fans, but it helped to replace the sense of purpose that Stephen had lost. And after a successful six-month run in London's theatre land, the singer finally realised he had found a more comfortable home for his theatrical talents than Boyzone had ever offered. Playing Joseph to an exuberant response from delighted audiences, Stephen's West End reputation was firmly established and the singer was presented with an opportunity to take a very different tack.

***

"I never thought a good soul like you would make a living out of scaring the living daylights out of children?" Elton quipped when the singer told him about the upcoming production of *Chitty Chitty Bang Bang*, in which he had been cast as the wicked Child Catcher.

"You've got to come along, I look hideously scary," enthused the baby-faced singer. "You won't even recognise me."

Wearing a skull-cap to appear bald and stick-on prosthetic ears and nose over a layer of heavy makeup, all to give him the sinister look the character required, Stephen stormed his way towards perhaps even more unlikely rave reviews once more. After all, although it wasn't the hard to imagine the baby-faced pop star as a convincing Joseph, it was much harder to envisage him as the wicked villain of the piece.

Night after night, from September 2004 to March 2005, from the moment he sauntered on stage his mere presence instantly drew loud applause from the crowd and Stephen milked every last ounce of it. It was hard to believe how his life had been transformed since lying in bed for days on end, ignoring any outside attempts of contact and popping pills just to keep himself going.

Gone was the zombie-like state, his inability to laugh or cry or feel any emotion, his nights spent with the curtains drawn as he stared for hours out his bedroom window. The stage had become his means of escape. Here he was, transported to a mystical world with pirates, castles, clever gadgets and mechanical contraptions to give him an outlet away from any demons he was wrestling in his head. He had become a real-life Peter Pan, breaking away from the dreariness of everyday life. He was glad to leap with the audience to a happier place, far away from anything that was happening in his everyday life.

Each night, as the magical car flew on stage for the first time within the show, audiences were captivated, stunned by the breathtaking effects. And Stephen, despite his dark role in the production, was transported with them.

The pantomime circuit later followed, and he played the role of Dandini in *Cinderella* in late 2005 and the Scarecrow in a production of *The Wizard of Oz* in Canterbury in early 2006. He also participated in a series of minor reality television shows, including Channel Five's *All Star Talent Show* and ITV's *Dancing on Ice*.

However, a few months later, he pulled of the UK tour of the musical *Godspell*, in which he was starring as Jesus, after just three weeks, blaming contractual problems. But a behind-the-scenes row had developed and the former boy band star left the rock opera after playing just two of its eight venues.

Gately, who was rumoured to be earning an impressive £12,000 a week to tour with the show around the UK, departed the production after a showdown with producer Paddy Wilson over poor ticket sales. It pained him that he couldn't pull in the audience and snide remarks that were going around West End social circles cut him deep. Newspapers reported that executives behind the Godspell tour assumed Stephen would be a big enough name to entice people to part with their cash and see a show. Stephen was gutted.

"They're saying Wilson thought I would make him the big bucks," he confided in his manager Louis Walsh. "That he thought my name would automatically sell out shows and it's all my fault that it's all falling apart," he sighed. "But it's not that simple."

"They're even questioning my performance now as Joseph," he said, his voice cracking with emotion. They said it wouldn't have been as big in the West End if the BBC hadn't given it millions of pounds worth of free publicity with the *Any Dream Will Do* TV casting show."

His manager reassured him, "Acting is a fickle game Stephen; your name will be back in lights in no time. You've got to have thicker skin."

But it wasn't the end of the bad run for Stephen.

A low-budget horror movie *Credo* followed and although the singer achieved a long held ambition – he always wanted to die in a slasher flick – the film never achieved any major commercial release or artistic recognition.

Stephen, on the crest of a wave just months earlier, began to sink back into self-doubt. He had worked so hard to rebuild his career. He had impressed the critics, sold out earlier shows, improved his acting, and all for what? He was beginning to feel that every time he scaled the dizzying heights of fame he would be kicked back down the golden ladder again before he even knew it was happening. And to make matters worse at the same time Stephen saw Ronan going from strength to strength.

Keating had performed for half a million people at the final concert of *Live 8*, and had even gone on to present the *MTV Europe Music Awards*, while his solo career was producing very respectable sales.

Meanwhile, as Stephen's career had been revived on the West End, another revival, this time of his love life, had taken place as well.

For several months between 2002 and 2003 Stephen would constantly moan to Elton that there were no eligible men on the scene and in turn Elton would become concerned as Stephen withdrew into himself after each stage production, favouring the comfort of a night alone rather than living it up like a typical celebrity on London's glitzy social circuit.

"Stephen, there's a charity bash this weekend and I want absolutely no excuses, you'll be there as if your life depended on it," Elton asserted. "There's someone I want you to meet." The singer was exhausted from the endless performances and dug his heels in but Elton being Elton wouldn't take no for an answer.

The night of the party Stephen turned up late and made his way through the star-studded collection of guests. His plan was to make an appearance and then head home early while the host entertained.

"Ah, you've finally graced us with your presence," Elton smiled. "And just in time too. Andy, I want to introduce you to someone."

A tall, suited stranger spun around to reveal a handsome and perfectly chiselled visage. His strong stubbled jaw line broke into a smile and his eyes twinkled at the sight of the Stephen. The baby-faced singer stood perfectly still, caught off-guard by the handsome vision before him.

"Nice to meet you," Andy Cowles introduced himself without breaking his gaze from Stephen's eyes. He offered his hand. Stephen

My front page exclusive in 2006 after Stephen told me how
he had slept with girl fans in the early days of Boyzone -
even though he knew he was gay.

Stephen and Andy enjoy a night on the town at the Meteor Awards in Dublin in 2006.

Jumping the gun, the Sunday People announced the Boyzone comeback was on thanks to Stephen Gately. They would have to wait another two years until Ronan could formally agree to return.

Stephen and his dance partner Kristina Lenko hit the ice on ITV's Dancing on Ice in 2007. Stephen admitted: "I was terrified of falling but I fell in love with it."

Stephen is my wing man as the Boyz ask me to practice
moves with them before their big comeback gig.

Stephen proudly shows me his new Superman tattoo in 2008.
After his death all his band mates got the same design inked
onto their arms in a touching tribute to him.

Lovers in arms. Stephen and Andy are inseparable
enjoy a night out in Ireland in 2008.

His last public appearance at the Pride Of Britain Awards
- Stephen was joined by Sharon Osbourne and PC Rachel
Farmer who won the emergency services award.

Stephen's holiday home in Majorca where he would spend his
final days and the shocking tragedy would unfold.

Back for their brother. The Mirror's front page as Stephen's band mates flew into Majorca in the aftermath of the tragedy.

A fitting send off from his Sheriff Street faithful.

Touching words for their hero. Fans left hundreds of floral
tributes outside the funeral service.

A forlorn fan pays her final respects to
Stephen at his funeral in October 2010.

Pain etched on their faces, Ronan, Mikey and Shane carry Stephen from the church.

Andrew is consoled outside the church, the pain is unbearable.

The lasting legacy.
Stephen's fantasy
book that would
only get completed
after his death.

felt like a teenager with his first crush. Something inside him leapt with excitement. "Hi I'm Andy, I've heard a lot about you."

He knew who Stephen was – in fact he used to have a teenage crush on him after seeing him on television several years earlier.

Elton left the pair to talk as they floated off into a quieter corner. Stephen was taken aback by the feelings Andy had awoken inside him. The connection was instant and the singer knew immediately it was something special. The next morning he rang Elton, babbling with excitement: "Wow, where have you been hiding him? He is absolutely gorgeous."

Elton laughed, "He is a computer entrepreneur. I knew he'd be right down your alley. Maybe he will bring you out of these fucking meal-for-one nights you've been having. It's about time you met someone nice."

A couple of weeks later, the pair met at another party. Afterwards, David Furnish began to play matchmaker.

"You should call Stephen. He really liked you," he encouraged.

But far from being the confident party animal he had appeared to be at that first meeting, Andrew was deep down a much shyer person. "No, I'm not going to," he insisted, "you don't just call someone out of the blue like that. He'll think it's weird'.

Nevertheless only a few weeks went by when fate had a part to play and Stephen bumped into the familiar face once more on the street. Andy had just been for a boozy lunch at the Ivy and recognised Stephen, who was shopping in Covent Garden.

"Would you fancy meeting for supper tomorrow night?" asked Andy.

The singer was embarrassed because he hadn't been prepared for the moment. He was unshaven and wore a beanie cap pulled down over his tired face. But he agreed nonetheless and the two arranged to meet up after Stephen's show. It was then that the romance took off.

"Go on, give us a couple of bars," encouraged Andy the following night as the two spent hours getting to know each other. "I want to hear what all the fuss is about." After a bit of goading, Stephen cleared his throat and nervously started to sing. He was used to performing to thousands of people. But this was different.

He swallowed the fear and broke the silence of their midnight romance; "*I Can Show You the World,*" he sang. "*Shinning, shimmering, splendid.*" Andy started to laugh. "I love Disney," he enthused, before joining in. The pair belted out the lyrics with all their heart, ignoring the idiocy of two grown men singing children's songs on their first date. It was as if they were the only two people on earth.

Andrew was 33 and worked in a technology company – Kapow – which provided text messaging services. He had flexibility in his job and his working life fitted in with Stephen's show business hours. The two became close very quickly, spending every ounce of free time together, and they quickly moved in together. It was the epitome of a whirlwind romance.

Andy would meet Stephen after his performances, and they would go for a late night meal in one of their favourite restaurants. Night after night, as the bistro emptied around them, they would laugh and talk and get to know each other.

Both came from large families that had come through poverty and conflict. Like Stephen, Andrew, whose home was near Bournemouth, Dorset, was also one of five – the second eldest. His bus-driver father married and divorced his mother twice before leaving them altogether, and Andrew endured a fractious upbringing, as he would tell Stephen while they pored over their lives with one another.

"He wasn't really there that often for any of us," Andy recalled. Looking at straight at Stephen, he smiled and said, "I think we're both a little damaged."

They spoke at length too about how their sexuality affected their earlier years. While Stephen had experienced a tough time with his parents since coming out, Andrew was a lot more comfortable about his sexual development. He had come out at 17, leaving home to do a BTEC in computer programming, before heading, at the age of 18, to London.

"The difference between us Stephen, is that you've got the whole Irish Catholic guilt thing going on," he would explain. "And you were put into a box for years in Boyzone simply because of your job. You were made to pretend to be somebody that just wasn't you. Your sexuality was always seen as a negative thing," he counselled.

But all that was behind them, and they were excited about the future. The both instinctively knew they had just found "the one".

On a whim they would jet to New York to spend long weekends together. When there, they had a favourite restaurant called Chez Josephine, where an old lady in her 90s named Sarah would sing the song *At Last* especially for the boys. Each time they returned they worried that she wouldn't be there because of her ageing years, never once considering that, in a cruel twist of fate, Andy would one day return without Stephen, and the old woman would sing the same romantic tune, reducing the heartbroken widower to tears.

But for now, they were still in the throes of young romance, and most nights they wouldn't get to bed until 2 a.m. When the morning sun came up, they would have breakfast together, read the papers, and then Andrew would leave for work.

But the long day dragged out in front of Stephen, as he wasn't on stage until much later that evening. So as Andy headed off to the office for a day's work, Stephen would watch cartoons like *SpongeBob SquarePants* before doing some household chores.

Andy would often arrive home to find a frustrated Stephen hoovering behind the sofa or mopping up the bathroom floor. He'd switch off the vacuum cleaner aggressively with a kick of his foot, "I've been doing the housekeeping all day," he'd protest. "You're never around to do your fair share. Just because I work nights doesn't mean I have to spend my days cleaning up after you. I need my free time too."

For the most part however, theirs was a happy union and after only a few weeks they had declared their undying love for one another.

One afternoon they were lying in each other's arms after another lazy day when Andy turned to Stephen and kissed him gently on the forehead. "Go on, marry me," he smiled. "What?" choked Stephen, shocked but delighted at the same time. "You heard me – marry me," laughed Andy. "You're fucking serious, aren't you?" Stephen replied, staring intently into his eyes.

After five months the pair flew to the city of blinding lights and made their way to the Chapel of Love in Las Vegas, where they held a commitment ceremony.

"I can't believe we're doing this," Stephen giggled, after declining Marylyn Monroe and Elvis Presley look-a-likes as witnesses. "Are we fucking mad?" he asked. "No babe, we're just in love," smiled Andy as he held him tightly. As they were leaving, the chapel played Etta James singing *At Last*. And it became their song.

Stephen and Andy didn't stay in Las Vegas for long, and after a shopping spree in Beverly Hills they flew back to London where they spent their honeymoon.

Friends were shocked but delighted. "You fucking what?" gasped Elton when Stephen called him after touching down. "David come here, guess who just got hitched!"

The couple made their first public appearance at Elton's famous "White Tie and Tiara Party", and their friends agreed they seemed as though they'd been an item for years, instead of just four months. Indeed the couple were already talking about adopting children.

Outside the world of showbiz, Stephen's biggest ambition was to adopt a child.

"My life will be complete once I have done that," he told Andy. "Now I have the chance to give my kids the best upbringing possible; the start in life I never had. They wouldn't have to worry about where the next meal was coming from," he went on. "And one day, I will be able to bring out the old Boyzone videos to show what daddy used to do," he laughed.

It was all plans for the future for the newly married couple, but Stephen's family weren't as enthused. "Stephen we barely even know the boy," his mother protested. The singer abruptly cut the conversation short. He wasn't in the mood for negativity and nothing was going to bring him down.

He had not visited his parents at home for several years. Even when his father needed 24-hour care after suffering a fall from a ladder, he steered clear of the family home. There was the odd phone call and he sent a bunch of red roses to his mother for her 50th birthday, but it would be many years before Stephen would finally return and build bridges once more.

In the meantime it was all systems go for the newly-weds. As the weeks went by they enjoyed gallivanting around and their lives had become filled with partying.

It was all building up to a spectacular moment when – only two months after their whirlwind Las Vegas wedding – their picture-perfect romance came crashing down in the most dramatic fashion.

The couple had just got back from Dublin after a long journey triggered by a cancelled flight and baggage problems, and went home to change before rushing out to dinner. They decided to hit the London hotspot, The Ivy, with two friends. In the heart of London's West End, it is a favourite haunt of celebrities such as Kate Moss and Naomi Campbell.

They enjoyed a romantic meal and a few sociable drinks but their night was only just getting started when all hell broke loose. Andy began chatting to another man and Stephen took exception to his friendliness. As shocked diners including George Michael looked on, the pair shouted at each other and the argument escalated until the two were asked by staff to leave the premises. Once outside the row quickly turned even nastier and a furious Andy launched an attack on Stephen.

"I don't care; you were out of order talking to him," shouted Stephen as the man in question disappeared down the street, leaving them to deal with their first real "domestic".

Andy's rage escalated and he let loose on the pint-sized star, punching and kicking him while passers-by stared on in shock and disbelief.

There was no chance that this could remain a private affair. That much they both knew. Paparazzi were never far away from The Ivy, but the row was so intense that as Stephen screamed under the volley of kicks and punches, a photographer named Greg Brennan – who was standing nearby taking the lucrative shots – couldn't bear to watch any more. "He was kicking him in the head, for God sake," he later recalled. The panicked photographer put down his camera and sprinted over to Stephen, "Get off him! Get the fuck off of him," he shouted, pulling Andy away from the battered singer.

Stephen looked terrified. He was shaking and got up off the ground as soon as he could escape. Worried onlookers tried to offer him help but he couldn't even talk to them; instead he ran back into the restaurant. Once in the toilet he locked the door behind him and broke down. He cried at the sight of his dishevelled state in the mirror as he tried to wash away the blood and clean up his face.

He was in complete shock. He loved Andy. But what was he thinking? What would his family and friends think once they saw the photographs? It was bound to get out. And he was right. The following day headlines screamed from newsstands about the terror the skinny singer had suffered at the hands of his new husband.

As he tried to deal with the media, Stephen slowly got back on speaking terms with Andy, who apologised profusely. But the damage had been done. What would everyone think?

Louis was one of the first people to call Stephen. He wanted to know if he was OK. He was furious at what happened. The singer was like a son to him and his manager would never let harm come his way.

"Stephen, is he always like this?" asked Louis. "It's bang out of order. I'll accept a lot of things that go on in your lives but this is not one of them."

"It's fine," Stephen sighed.

"Fine? How could it be fine," Louis shot back. He had promised himself he wouldn't lose his cool but he felt Stephen needed a wake-up call. "He hit you Stephen," he exclaimed. "He hit you! In the middle of a busy street. If he's doing that in public what sort of thing is he doing behind closed doors?"

"You know what it's like; men fight, Louis," he reassured his boss. "It only lasted a few minutes. We don't really know what happened. It was over something really stupid but I just can't remember much of it. We were very tipsy and tired. It's not fair as I hit him first and he's getting the blame for whacking me," Stephen insisted. "For crying out loud I started it."

Once Stephen had made attempts to reassure Louis, they began working on a defence against the media backlash. The horror in showbiz circles was palpable and this wasn't something that was going to go away any time soon. For his part, Louis told Stephen that if it ever happened again, that would have to be the end of their relationship. Back in Ireland, the singer's family were horrified.

Meanwhile, the couple went shopping together on Bond Street and popped into Cartier to see if their wedding rings were ready to be collected. All the while the media were stunned that Stephen would stay in the relationship after such a vicious incident.

"We are very happily married and have just bought a house. We're moving in soon and are very serious about each other," Stephen insisted. "Andrew isn't nasty, he's a sweet guy and we love each other so much."

Andy also did his part to play the incident down, "We have never hit each other before. It was just a tipsy bitch-slap situation. There definitely wasn't any blood – it was just lip-gloss," he laughed, trying to make light of the incident as concerned friends continued to inundate Stephen with calls.

The singer also posted a message to his fans on his official website that read: "Andy and I were papped in London having a disagreement and I'm aware that unfortunately it may not look particularly pretty. Obviously I would have preferred this not to become public but I wanted you to hear directly from me that Andy and I are absolutely fine."

***

As with everything in the fast-paced world of show business, the public spat was soon forgotten and privately their relationship strengthened as they tried to put the drama behind them. They moved into their new house in North London. They spent £1.5 million on the six bedroom mansion and soon made it their home, moving in Andrew's sister and two big dogs. They even had a housekeeper five days a week, so they could get on with their working lives.

Although happily married and at the top of his game, Stephen still displayed some childhood vulnerabilities. If he was working away, even if he was as far away as Birmingham or Manchester, he would go home to Andy rather than stay in a hotel.

"Stephen, you'll be exhausted if you make the drive now," Andy would say to him after his late nights but Stephen was adamant. "I want to come home and see you babe, I hate being away," he would say.

Indeed even as a well-travelled star Stephen still held on to his childish ways. He loved spending his evenings watching Disney movies and playing board games and would often play practical jokes on Andy.

On the flip side, he was scared of being alone, scared of the dark, and scared that he might become poor once more – like his parents. It was one part of his childhood he definitely didn't want to revert to.

"I don't know," he would tell Andy. "I'm just always terrified I'll end up back on Sheriff Street. I never want to go back there again."

But his husband would brush it off with his usual reassurance. "Stephen, a lot of things might happen to you. But that is definitely not one of them," he laughed. "Sure, aren't we going to retire at 40? And I'm making sure too that we will have a secure future."

The relationship between them was underpinned by their well-suited needs. Andy had spent most of his teenage life helping his mother raise his younger siblings, while Stephen knew he needed to be looked after.

Brown envelopes would come through the door on a daily basis - only to be cast aside by Stephen.

"Stephen it's a bill! You never even bothered opening it," Andy would remonstrate.

The singer looked at him apologetically and shrugged. But Andy couldn't be annoyed. He knew exactly where Stephen was coming from. Stephen had come from being a confused and penniless teenager on the back streets of Dublin, and now found himself earning vast sums of money each month, without having to worry about paying bills and doing mundane errands.

"Those things were always done by someone else when I was in the band," came his innocent reply. "I'm not used to it."

It was something Andy took over once they married. Stephen needed to be cared for and cherished and Andy needed someone he could take care of. Despite the ghastly incident outside The Ivy, they were both good for one another.

Even if his family couldn't see it at the time. Stephen's mother and father were left reeling by the incident outside the Ivy. His mother, in particular, was worried for her son and the type of relationship he had found himself in. But she couldn't articulate her feelings to him after years of estrangement. And when he realised his dreams and eventually wed the love of his life, Stephen's mom would sadly be missing from the photo.

CHAPTER EIGHT
Unions and Reunions

It had been many years since the fateful interview that ended Stephen's relationship with his mother. She had spoken to a newspaper when he first announced he was gay and unwittingly said some things that Stephen took issue with.

"I'm '... not a paedophile...'– she said that, Louis?" He laughed in disbelief as he relayed her words to his manager after the article hit the stands. "I never asked to be gay! That's implying that there is something wrong with it! How could she be so thoughtless?"

Since then things had never been the same between them.

Margaret had tried to keep in touch but her son's head was more stubborn than his heart was forgiving and their communication had been pared down to strained telephone calls and barbed comments, mostly on Stephen's behalf.

His mother was a kind soul who always wanted what was best for her son. If she could turn back the hands of time from when she heard that fateful knock on the door of her small Dublin home, she would have done so, a million times over.

She thought time would heal all wounds. She certainly never believed he would be this angry and resentful all these years later.

But he was. And it cut her to the core.

He sat in silence for a moment as he heard Andy come in. "you alright babe?"

"Ah yeah I'm just thinking about my mother," Stephen sighed.

He collapsed on the couch as his husband came over and sat beside him.

"I don't understand," Stephen looked exasperated. "Why can't she just be happy for me? After all these years? She knows how long it's taken me to get here. I put my heart and soul into this business. And she knows how cut up I was after Eloy until I met you," Andy put his arm around him.

"I'm finally happy Andy," he continued. "For the first time in my life I can finally say I've found everything I'm looking for and she can't so much as pick up the phone and tell me she's happy for me."

It was a sentiment Stephen would carry with him for many years to come. As he and Andy grew in love, the pop star grew more and more distant from his family.

Although they weren't in contact for months on end, his mother kept her love alight for her son by entertaining fans when they called at her door. She would bring them in for tea and sandwiches by the half dozen. She would listen wistfully as she heard them relay their stories about her son.

How they spotted him walking down Dublin's Grafton Street

one day and he had spent fifteen minutes chatting to them before giving them a picture, how he had signed a school shirt for one of the girls which still hung on her bedroom wall and how well he was doing for himself on the West End.

She loved hearing these stories, but sometimes they filled her heart with sadness. It seemed she now lived for her son only through his fans. The boy she nursed as a newborn, the son she had soothed asleep when he was afraid of the dark, the child she put her arms around when he came home crying after being teased in the street.

He was no longer hers – he was theirs – and although she was so proud of all he had achieved, a big part of her was aching to reclaim him as her own.

For Stephen however, the detachment from his family, especially his mother, and the void that left in his heart, was being filled by his ever-strengthening relationship with Andy.

They had even discussed having children of their own.

"I want to adopt, babe," he said to Andy one morning, stroking his hair as they were lying in bed. "I think I would make a great dad. I know you would too. I'm serious; I really want us to look into it."

For Stephen having a son or daughter to call his own was a dream that hadn't materialised during his failed relationship with Eloy, but now he was sure he had finally met the right man to raise children with.

"Well we better make it official in Britain first," reasoned Andy.

He was full of Stephen's enthusiasm but of the two he was the more rational. "Let's get the civil union here. It's the first step." And so the preparations got underway in earnest.

On 19 March 2006, two days after Stephen turned 30, the pair's love for one another was finally official on British soil. Wearing designer suits, they looked picture-perfect as they gazed at each other hand in hand.

"Why am I so nervous when we've done this all before," whispered Stephen, laughing quietly as they stood in front of family and friends

"Because it's as exciting as the first time round," replied Andy. "And we're even more sure than ever that we're perfect for each other," he smiled as Stephen's eyes lit up with delight.

It was exactly as he had always imagined it. They had dug deep for their special day; spending in the region of €60,000 on the festivities. But ever since Stephen realised that his love knew no bounds, he wanted to lay on the finest celebration for their big day, and money was no object.

The Goring Hotel was an oasis in the city where they had spent much time. With its private gardens and Edwardian dining rooms it offered the perfect location for the pair to share their vows.

Stephen became emotional as they exchanged wedding bands. When he was a young boy he could have never imagined that he would be slipping a €20,000 diamond and platinum wedding ring onto another man's finger, so happily and openly in front of his closest friends. Let alone that he would be putting it on the hand of a man that he knew was his one true soul mate, the person he wanted to grow old and raise children with.

All of his dreams had come together in this one blissful moment. He could barely contain his emotion as he looked into Andy's eyes, sensing his partner's devotion. What followed was a lavish reception beyond anything the guests had ever seen before. Flowers and candles adorned every table and Cristal Champagne flowed freely among celebrities and friends as they toasted the happy couple.

"Darling, you look fabulous," a flamboyant Elton John said as he swanned towards them. He threw his arms around Stephen and studied him closely. "My how far you've come," he said, holding him tight. The two were lost for words as they hugged, all too aware of the journey Elton had helped him through.

"I don't know what to say," said Stephen as he broke the embrace and looked his mentor in the eye. But the colourful legend stopped him in his tracks. "Don't... say... one... word," he ordered, spelling out each syllable and pushing his finger to his lips. "Seeing you two here today is enough. That's all the thanks I need."

Stephen thanked him and turned to walk away, but Elton turned towards him again: "Actually...now that you mention it... that sexed up painting that you got David and me after your last wedding? It went down a storm," he recalled, referring to the homoerotic painting Stephen and Andy had presented them with after their Las Vegas nuptials. "David and I can't wait to see what you've done to top that," he clapped as he sauntered off into the crowd.

Stephen mingled with guests to the sound of the orchestra as another celebrity friend made her way over, "Stephen," squealed a pint-sized blonde in a tight fitting dress. It was Spice Girl Emma Bunton. "Get over here you bugger! That should have been me putting that ring on your finger," she laughed as she threw her arms around him.

Elsewhere amid the excited buzz of conversation, Graham Norton and George Michael turned heads as they chatted to guests between courses.

But in between all the delicate flower arrangements and air-kisses, Stephen knew deep that two things were missing. And they were two of the things he considered most important in his life – whether he liked to admit it or not. He excused himself and went into the plush private bathroom to escape the madness of the celebrations.

As he looked in the mirror at the man he had become that familiar twinge of guilt wrenched through his gut. He hadn't even told his mother about his big day. He had wrestled with the thought on so many occasions but he just couldn't bring himself to do it. After all she had said about Andy, all the concerns she expressed, would she even have wanted to come?

But he knew that wasn't the point. The reality was she would see her son splashed across the front pages of the newspapers the next day. It would be there before her in black and white that she had missed out on another major milestone in his life – and that her son had wanted it that way.

Still he couldn't bring himself to heal the rift. He loved his mother dearly and he knew she loved him. But theirs was a stubborn relationship and it would take some time before they could work things out.

***

There was, however, another great love of his life that was missing that day. And although it would be difficult, if not impossible to achieve, he had a burning desire to fix it. Indeed Stephen felt that with a bit of time and effort he might just stand a chance of putting things right.

He wanted Boyzone back together again. Sure there were a few obstacles in the way. For one, there was still a lot of bad feeling between Ronan and Keith. Stephen remembered how Keith had voiced his anger at Ronan so many times over the years since the group split. Keith had always felt Ronan forced them to break up so he could pursue a solo career. And Ronan had said there was no going back because of the fallout. But even still, Stephen felt it was worth a shot.

The desire had been building up inside him ever since he saw UK boy band Take That reunite. Ten years after they first split, they managed to put their differences aside and they even proved that they didn't need Robbie Williams to get back on track. Surely this was a wakeup call for the lads?

His first port of call was Ronan. "If I get him on board it would be half the battle," he told Andy. He picked up the phone to his old band mate and tentatively floated the idea, taking care not to seem too pushy. But even so, Ronan was quick to pour cold water on the flame.

"Steo, some horrible things were said about me man. I can't just forget all that shit. It's gone too far now," Ronan told him. "It's not going to happen."

It had been Ronan's idea that they should take a breather after years of touring, six Number one hits and sales of 11 million records. He had embarked on a solo career and hadn't come back. Ever since, the rest of the group had floundered in limbo, uncertain whether they would ever reform.

For his part, Ronan went down a storm with solo hits like *Life is a Rollercoaster* and *Tomorrow Never Comes*. He had proven to himself that he could do it alone and was in no mood to share the spotlight with four other guys. Especially when some of them had badmouthed him to the press.

"Come on mate," Stephen reasoned on a later attempt to win Ronan round. He had lost count of the number of fruitless calls he had made to the singer at this stage. "Think about it. If Boyzone get back together we could sell out every major arena in Ireland and the UK. We went out at our peak. The fans are still gagging for us. They've stayed as loyal as ever. They're literally sitting, waiting for us to release another album, launch another tour, whatever, just so they can snap it all up.

"It's never going to be about the money, it's about the music. I know that," he continued, "But you can't deny the fact that we're still capable of making the big bucks. The tough bit is getting all you fuckers to stop being so stubborn about it," he laughed. As time went by he could sense Ronan coming around to the idea – slowly but surely.

Weeks later he thought he had hit the jackpot when a multi-millionaire tycoon offered the band €1 million to reunite and play at his wedding.

"Ronan this guy is minted, his wife-to-be is a massive fan, and money is no object. What do you say?" But his former band mate still was having none of it, even with a share of a million sitting on the table. If anything showed how far the band had travelled since their Transit van touring days, that moment might have captured it better than any.

By this stage Stephen had convinced Shane, Keith, and Mikey to put their differences aside. But this made no difference to the biggest Boyzone star.

"I told you the answer is no," replied Ronan. "I still want to give my full focus to my solo career and money is irrelevant. It won't change my mind. I just can't see us performing together on a stage again after everything that's happened."

Stephen could feel his own frustration rise. The other lads would be furious. It was an easy €200,000 each for an hour's work but Ronan didn't need the money and wasn't budging.

"What do you mean he said no," shouted Keith in disbelief when Stephen relayed the bad news. "Is he for fucking real? Does he really have that much money that he can turn his nose up at something like that," he snapped. "He fucking held the rest of us back when he went off to do his solo shite. And he's doing the same thing now. Some things never change. Its times like this I'm fucking glad we split. I can't believe I thought for a second that he'd even think about considering the rest of us," he shouted. "Pure selfish."

It looked like it was never going to happen. There were even days when Stephen felt that the more he tried to make things happen, the more he pushed the others further apart.

"I don't know if it's worth it," he confided to Andy, incensed that his efforts were amounting to nothing. "I just feel like I'm opening up old wounds. I'm dragging up the past. Maybe I should just let sleeping dogs lie."

"Keith's getting on well with the *Coronation Street* gig, Shane and Mikey have never been happier with reality shows and writing music and Ronan, sure he has this solo thing happening now. He's making big waves out there. What would he want to reunite for at this stage? Maybe the split was for the best."

But Andy wasn't buying it. "You can't give up on it Steo. The rest of the lads are relying on you. They may be stubborn; they may have a bit of pride to swallow yet. But deep down I know they all want this to happen. And they need you to make it happen. You're the lynch-pin of the group," he continued. "You always held it all together. But apart from all that, I know that you, more than anyone else, wants this reunion to happen. So you should go after it with everything you've got – even if it's with your own dreams in mind."

Stephen knew he was right and eventually his persistence paid off, with a little helping hand from fate. Along came an ultimatum that would save the day. A promoter had put an extremely appealing offer on the table. He rang Louis and outlined the lucrative deal. There was only one catch.

"They must agree within the month," he said. "It's now or never. No pussyfooting about this time OK?"

Stephen rang Ronan once more, "Well, what's it going to be?"

He knew instantly by the long silence that Ronan's resistance was crumbling at last and that something big was about to happen. Gone were the protestations, the excuses. In the end, all the reasoning in the world couldn't quench the burning desire, once the spark had been lit, to perform again to sold-out arenas around the country. And Stephen could feel it in the air. Ronan's zest for the big-time had been ignited once more.

Weeks later they were sitting around a table in Dublin – just like old times. They had invited Louis along too. And he had some patching up to do with Ronan after their falling out over comments he made during the singer's solo career. When Louis had compared him to Irish performer Daniel O'Donnell – a favourite among grandmothers – Ronan had been furious and sacked Louis, who he said had no interest in his career.

"And I'm sorry for saying you should be the new Cliff Richard too," Louis said sheepishly. "It was more tongue in cheek than anything," he shrugged with a twinkle in his eye. I have the habit of opening my mouth and not thinking. I can't help it," he smiled. "Sometimes I do think: 'Oh God why did I say that?' But anyways, at the time it sounded funny," he laughed.

"Louis it's behind us. You've been like a father to me though the years," said Ronan, "And anyway, I've sold enough singles now since going solo that I don't take it so much to heart anymore," he smirked.

Pints were poured and issues ironed out as the boys stepped up to the plate and talked through their differences.

"I'd like to give people the concert they never got," offered Shane.

"We always said at the end of our concerts we would be back the next year and then we weren't. Even if we just had a massive gig, just to make amends for that broken promise, then that would be a great way to say thank you to everyone."

The lads agreed. And by December 2006 they had signed along the dotted line.

At the time Take That was storming the charts with their single *Patience*, and it gave the lads the belief they needed that they too could make it back to the top of the pile.

"We've already got a head start," quipped Ronan. "At least we're all coming back together. No one doing stints in rehab here," he laughed.

The boys began talks with ITV to do an hour-long documentary to coincide with their re-launch and quickly began taking it far more seriously than they ever did during their earlier career. Gone was the mismatched wardrobe and laissez-faire attitude. With new pop bands from America saturating the market, they knew they had to up their game.

"Singing practise, diet, gym, the whole shebang," outlined Gately as their training rehearsal schedule began in preparation for the launch of the tour in Belfast. "And dancing classes – we'll be doing more dancing than we've ever done before."

His enthusiasm was contagious. He reminded them of the important things about the reunion. Money wasn't an issue now – they were all very comfortable so they needed another kind of motivation.

"If you think about it lads, when we were younger we were so concerned about trying to crack the market that we could never really enjoy it," he reasoned.

Louis had organised a 24-date tour, which they would officially unveil to fans after their first big comeback performance, which had been secured for the Children In Need show on BBC 1. It would be a mammoth opportunity to return with a bang in front of tens of millions of viewers. But first they needed to get into shape.

"I want to sex up this tour," Louis ordered as he outlined his plans to make them number one once more. I want you guys to out-sex Take That," he asserted.

"You what," laughed Stephen, sounding instantly intrigued.

"You heard me," replied Louis. "You're stripping to your underwear on the first night of the live tour," he announced.

The lads broke out in stitches of laughter. They had listened to a lot of their eccentric manager's crazy ideas over the years but this had to take the biscuit.

"Louis in case you hadn't noticed, we're not exactly bronzed muscle men," laughed Stephen.

"Correction," came the reply. "You're not bronzed Adonis's... YET."

"You've got a promotional photo shoot, recreating the magic moment from the movie *The Full Monty* in one of the glossy magazines...*HEAT*," said Louis. "You better make sure you're all fit or you're going to be an even bigger laughing stock than the night I threw you in the deep end on *The Late Late*."

The tour Director, who was standing nearby sizing the lads up, concurred. "You're all going to have to lose some weight and get in shape or we're going to have to pull all the dance routines. "They're a lot trickier than anything you've ever done before, and we're adding 12 backing dancers to your on-stage routine. If Take That can do it, so can you."

"Come on lads," he laughed lightening the mood, "don't look so worried. You're going to have half-naked dancers gyrating around you. It's going to be brilliant."

Louis rubbed his hands together. He was relishing the challenge. "We're gonna kick Take That outta the water. Let's reclaim the limelight guys."

Boyzone had a lot to live up to. Take That's tour was a sell-out and their new album, *Beautiful World*, was one of the most successful releases in the UK in 2007.

But the boys were not fazed.

***

For three solid months they worked, choreographing dance routines from seven in the morning: "And take it from the top," the choreographer would scream as sweat dripped down their faces in the dance studio. "And again, and again, and again. Until it's absolutely perfect," he clapped.

After each song, they would scrape themselves off the polished wooden floors, line up side by side in the full length mirrors and start from scratch again until the routine was absolutely flawless. And when perfection was achieved they'd start all over again on the next number. Every day it seemed that something new was wheeled out to let the lads know this was going to be like nothing they'd ever worked on before.

"You want us to trot topless on treadmills?" laughed Stephen in disbelief. He was loving the idea a bit more than the others. "Yes," shrugged the director, "like boxers in training," he said without batting an eyelid.

The boys looked uncertainly at each other, waiting to see who'd be the first to throw in the towel. But before they even had a chance, Stephen had hopped on one of the machines.

"Come on lads," he laughed switching it on. "You can cut down your gym time. Two birds with the one stone."

Indeed when they weren't dancing they were working out. The band had been introduced to a Dublin fitness instructor called Paul Byrne, who promised to transform their shape.

"We've only got 12 weeks boys," he stressed. "I'll give it my all but you've got to work with me here. You've got to cut out the booze, clean up your diet and lift weights until your muscles are ripped. Pain is imperfection leaving the body," he smiled, his huge torso giving them an idea of the pain they were about to be put through.

And after three months of intense discipline and training all their hard work had paid off.

A huge team from the magazine had gathered for the first photo shoot. Louis watched expectantly from the wings and a team of stylists, make-up artists and lighting experts jostled for space in the cramped white stark white studio floor. The band stood before the curtain looking sheepish and embarrassed.

"Don't be shy lads, come on out," called one of the magazine staff. A couple of the younger girls giggled. One by one, they all lined up under the hot studio lights in front of the glittering gold streamers.

Silence fell on the production team as they waited for the moment of truth. The girls in the production team pushed aside their male colleagues, grabbing their mobile phones to text their jealous friends about the sight they were about to behold. But even they couldn't have imagined the reaction to the new sexed-up look that proved that months of hard work and self sacrifice had paid off.

There were gasps of disbelief as the new Boyzone look was unveiled. Each and every one of them had somehow been chiselled into leaner, more muscular visions of their former selves.

"My oh my," laughed someone from behind the cameras. "Would you looky here."

The boys glanced at each other nervously as they laughed at their newfound admirers. They had nothing on but black top hats, strategically placed to protect their dignity. And they didn't look ridiculous, as all of them had feared they would when Louis first came up with the idea.

All of them, bar Mikey, displayed newly acquired tattoos that added to their new grown-up look. They smiled confidently as the females in the room soaked up the view.

"Forget what Tom Jones said lads," yelled a girl from the back. "You can get rid of the hats!" The room erupted with an excited round of applause and enough hollering and wolf whistling to confirm that Louis had made another great call. With or without top hats, the lads were back with a bang.

CHAPTER NINE
The Boyz are Back

Stephen composed himself and turned his back to the gigantic screens that were displaying imposing images of each of his band mates. Behind him he could hear a murmur of quiet anticipation in the *BBC Children In Need* audience, swiftly broken by a floor manager screaming out the final frantic cues to his busy army of cameramen, sound engineers and runners. "One minute to Boyzone," he beckoned. "Cue the lights."

He had been here a thousand times before, but this time he was trembling. It was November 17 2007 – but it was just like all those years ago on the *Late Late Show*, only they weren't teenagers anymore. Now in their thirties, they had to prove themselves all over again and it felt every bit as daunting as that night in the RTE studios. Seven years he had waited for this moment, but Stephen couldn't help but feel everyone was waiting to see them fail. There was only one thing better than a comeback, as far as the press were concerned, and that was a flawed comeback.

Dressed in black trousers and shirt, Stephen looked to his left for a nod of reassurance. But Keith Duffy's face was transfixed ahead of him, his forehead furrowed in stern concentration. Panic stricken, he glanced to his right, but there was no help there either. Next to him was Mikey, then Ronan and last in the line, Shane. They all stared ahead impassively, each contending with their own private emotions, fears and anxieties as they waited for that screen to roll back and reveal them in all their splendour.

Stephen brushed his sweaty palms over his trousers, fearing he would drop the microphone as soon as he grabbed it. Taking deep breaths the final cue came and the screens rolled back. Pure instinct took over as they all turned to face the audience in unison, took three long strides towards the microphones and burst into song.

Stephen, after an emotional journey of self doubt and rediscovery, had finally arrived home. His head was swirling with a realm of emotions, but somehow he had to keep a lid on it or their big comeback could be blown in front of 17 million TV viewers before it had even got off the ground. Stephen took a final glance out to the audience, fixed his gaze into camera three and brazenly took the lead vocals, bursting into their number one hit and anthem *No Matter What*.

The camera panned over the specially selected audience, some of whom looked more than a little out of place with their charity banners and Pudsey the Bear teddies. But Stephen was in no doubt that the real audience were beyond the confines of the BBC studios in London, feeling assured that his every smile and wink, timed perfectly as the cameras panned across him, would reach nearly every living room in the land.

Maybe it was the nerves, because God knows they'd had enough time to rehearse, but their performance was far from the flawless, polished display that they may have dreamed of during all those dormant years when a Boyzone comeback was pie in the sky.

Stephen grimaced slightly as he dropped a couple of flat notes, and even the normally perfect Ronan appeared vocally strained as he took the lion's share of the lead singing duties.

While so many things had changed since they last took to the stage, little had altered in the dynamics of the group. It was immediately clear that Stephen and Ronan would carry the other three members, throwing enough smoke and mirrors into the equation to distract from the clumsy routines and unsophisticated dance moves. Keith, with his new found gym regime and tanning, may have looked like something out of a muscleman competition, but the hulking physique did little to lend itself to the spins, glides and nimble gestures that had been worked into their choreography. Shane looked slightly embarrassed to be back on stage singing teen pop songs while Mikey, despite his superior vocal range, still looked every bit the odd one out with his fatherly image and uncool hairstyle.

To the casual viewer the whole performance may have looked laboured and gimmicky, but Stephen knew that none of that mattered tonight. There would be plenty of time to polish up on those things later, during the rehearsals for their dazzling multi-date tour, which should sell by the bucket load given their priceless piece of self-promotion. Six minutes and twenty seconds later it was all over. Seven years in the making and, as far as the boys could tell from the jubilant response from the audience, they had pulled off mission impossible.

Terry Wogan dashed over to grab Stephen's hand, which by now was raised in a triumphant fist, as if he'd just delivered a knockout blow to Muhammad Ali. Unlike the RTE host Gay Byrne on that infamous night in Dublin during their first ever TV appearance, there was no castigating or ridicule this time. "Boy are they glad to see you back or what!" Wogan graciously exclaimed to the millions watching on TV. "It's wonderful for you to come together and do this."

Stephen jumped up and down like a child on Christmas morning as Ronan announced that they were touring again, and that the tickets would be on sale first thing on Monday morning. Then the pretty presenter Holly Willoughby turned to Stephen. How did that feel?" she asked. "It was incredible, I loved it," he exclaimed giddily, again jumping up and down.

As they dashed back to their dressing room, champagne bottles were uncorked, hugs and kisses were being exchanged between the delighted Boyzone WAGS, and even Louis Walsh couldn't contain his excitement. "Everyone is going to want tickets for this tour," he promised. "We're back boys and it's going to be huge." But it was clear for all to see that this comeback meant more to Stephen than anyone. While others in the group may have been eyeing up a tidy pay day, Stephen's motivations couldn't have been further from monetary matters.

As the jubilant scenes erupted around him, Stephen burst out of the room to find Andy – the man who had guided him with love and encouragement back to the light. This was a moment so sweet, so precious, that he wanted to share it with the man he loved. When they finally found each other amid the mayhem of the BBC studios, Andy barely even had to say a word. He put his arms around Stephen and whispered: "Well done baby. You did it. I'm so proud of you."

***

Yet there was still something missing. As the Boyzone comeback wagon burst into full speed ahead, Stephen had some unfinished business to attend to. He knew that without making amends with his family back in Dublin, it would all be meaningless. What was the point in completing the journey back to his roots without the very people that helped him get there in the first place?

The truth was that Stephen's differences with his parents had been played out for a mind- numbingly long period. What should have been a disagreement had boiled over into an all out family feud. He had allowed what could have easily just have been a blip in their relationship to overtake them. The result was months of stubborn silence between them until, tired and perplexed by Stephen's stand-off, his brother Mark called him up and told him in no uncertain terms to sort it out. "Look, this whole situation can't last forever. Life's too short Stephen, get over here and see mum and dad," he warned his brother with authority.

Andy agreed that Stephen needed to reconcile with his parents, for himself as much as anyone else. Stephen admitted he had left it so long that he was nervous about returning to the streets where he grew up. "It's like it's a different world to me now," he said. "What if I turn up there and mam doesn't want to speak to me?" Andy replied, "That's not going to happen. She is your mother Stephen; she loves you no matter what."

The following day Stephen and Andy arrived at the small mid-terrace home that his parents still lived in. There were no awkward silences or stern words, just loving embraces and a humble apology from Stephen: "I'm sorry for leaving it so long," he told them. "I was being stubborn and silly and I want you to know I love you." It was a massive weight off his shoulders, and he felt angered at himself that he had let it drag on so long in the first place.

Stephen spent the day showing Andy around his old stomping grounds, walking the humble streets that he'd grown up on and feeling a new sense of pride about his home town. "I sometimes forget how much I love this place," he told Andy. "It's like a part of me still belongs here. We have to come back more often."

Stephen returned to London buoyed by his reconciliation with his family. Suddenly all the pieces in the jigsaw were falling into place. He had longed for so long to rediscover the true sense of inner contentment that only music and Boyzone had ever delivered him, and now the stars were aligning in his favour.

***

Away from the full throttle of a monumental Boyzone comeback, Stephen and Andy were settling into a domestic bliss in London. They had put their savings together to splash out on a luxurious £1.5 million, four bedroom home in trendy Highgate, which they decorated with the finest furnishings and artwork.

The pair spent their evenings in the local Red Lion pub or sipping champagne in Flutes wine bar, meeting friends at their leisure. They could also enjoy anonymity in an area whose residents were well used to seeing celebrities on the streets. Among their neighbours were George Michael, Ray Davies and the actress Julia Stephenson.

One evening, their idyll was briefly shattered when they returned from a short break away to find their belongings ransacked by an intruder. Among the burglar's haul was expensive jewellery and sound systems. But typically, Stephen was more hurt by the loss of the treasured watch which he had bought himself with his first Boyzone paycheque.

Enraged and spurred to action, he picked up the phone to his local newspaper, *The Hampstead* and *Highgate Express*, to warn his neighbours and appeal for the return of his property. "I can't believe how much they took," he said, clearly saddened by the drama. "I don't mind about the other stuff – I can replace all that. But the watch was very dear to my heart, because when Boyzone got our first paycheques we all bought watches to celebrate and it was very special to me. It feels like someone has stolen a piece of my past."

As the Boyzone PR machine went into overdrive to sell out their ambitious run of arena dates, Stephen turned his attention to matters of the body. He and his band mates were now heavily into the gym and proudly packing impressive figures after dozens of personal training sessions with Dublin trainer-to-the-stars Paul Byrne. Keith wanted to take their Full Monty shoot one step further and flash their new killer bodies live on stage: "What if we get in shape then we'll do a number with our tops off on stage. We'll get an amazing reaction and we'll show people that we can still hold our own against those young lads," he brazenly suggested. Stephen was happy to play along: "We're in. Let's give ourselves two months to get in the shape of our lives – we'll show all those people who say we're over the hill. Lets tell everyone we're coming out meaner and leaner than ever before."

A few days later Ronan hinted at their big plan to use their bodies as their biggest weapons as the band hit the publicity trail. Little did fans realise the plan had been hatched thanks to Stephen's conversation with Keith just nights before. "We've been taking it easy on the Guinness and been out for dinners and just a couple of drinks," he said, somewhat misleadingly. "We're taking the tour plans very seriously. We're all on diets and we've been training in the gym every day. I'm probably the fittest now that I've ever been. I think we all look better now than before." Continuing to set the bar perilously high, Ronan added: "We each went to see Take That on tour at different times and started talking to each other again, but Take That were the icing on the cake that made us decide now was the time to reform. We're very aware of how good Take That are, and we know we have to be on a par with them. There won't be a flat, boring stage. We're all dancing again and learning different things we've never done before to rival their pole dancing and stuff."

As their May 25 opening night date with destiny in Belfast approached, Stephen was in exhilarating form. When Louis hired a team of dancers, a full-on 8-piece band and a top live show producer to make their comeback the greatest in pop, it was clear that this would not be a "token tour" that would rely on dining out on past glories. Stephen put his heart and soul into every rehearsal, waking at 7 a.m. each morning to go to the gym and pump iron, then hitting the dance lessons that were mercilessly staged for three hours before lunch and four hours after

"I'm absolutely exhausted," he said as the rehearsals grew in intensity as they neared the opening night. "But at the same time I've never felt so alive. I'm living a really healthy lifestyle, I'm watching what I eat and I go to the gym six days a week. The bottom line is we have to be 100 per cent ready when those lights go up in Belfast – we can't let the fans down because they've wanted this as much as we have. So I'm giving my everything to rehearsals and hopefully the fans will see the results when we hit the stage.

***

Before long their evening of reckoning was upon them. Outside Belfast's polished Odyssey Arena, fans milled about in the warm evening sunshine, parading around in pink cowboy hats, flashing bunny ears and tee-shirts proclaiming their undying love for each member of the band. Inside was a starkly less carefree atmosphere, as the blunt realisation of a make-or-break sell-out show stood before them. The wild abandonment and joking that had carried them through rehearsals was now replaced with a reticent, even sombre sense of the foreboding.

At the far end of a long, white-walled corridor, a pair of light oak double doors opened to reveal a gigantic square room filled with their stage costumes, a music player and, rather bizarrely, a spray tanning system. When I arrived at their backstage compound with Louis, even Ronan's wife Yvonne was availing herself of the perks of life on a boy band tour, pulling on a white dressing gown after getting a quick pre-show spray down. In a corner of the room was

Stephen, who looked like he had gotten lost on his way home from a beauty spa, wearing a white face mask that made him look like an extra from the *Thriller* video. Then he suddenly leapt up and turned the sound system to the highest volume as he went through his final steps to a medley of their biggest hits.

It was clear for anyone with the band that night to see who Louis thought deserved the credit for the successful reunion. "You made it happen Stephen, you made it happen kid," he told him, grabbing him by the arm as their production manager announced there were just ten minutes before stage time. "You were the one who brought this all together – if it wasn't for you I wouldn't have done it. So we all owe you a big thanks." For Stephen the earnest words from Louis instantly validated all the anger and frustration he had endured trying to make this moment a reality.

But there was little time for sentiment when 10,000 screaming fans were waiting for the boys to deliver. Almost as soon as Louis had let go of Stephen's arms the other band members – Keith, Shane, Ronan and Mikey burst through the doors in a frenzy of excitement.

Dressed in tight silver trousers and skimpy tee-shirts, it seemed the boys were happier than ever to camp it up, perhaps realising, now with a new maturity, that Stephen's sexuality was an asset to be embraced and used to generate every last pink pound possible. Stephen placed himself at the middle of an emotional embrace with the others, hugged his partner Andy, turned and marched to the back of the stage where they could already hear the deafening cries of their eager die-hard fans from behind the screens.

With perfect timing, a blast of Thin Lizzy's *The Boys Are Back in Town* reverberated out of the PA system, sending the hoards of females in the audience into hysterics. As anticipation hit fever pitch a space shuttle-style countdown climaxed, with their squad of sexy female dancers standing in a circle and pointing neon rods skywards. Suddenly, amid a dazzling volley of explosions, Stephen stepped out on top of a staircase to send the front rows into dreamland as the opening bars of *Picture of You* rang out over the arena. Each member of the band broke into broad smiles as the realisation of their tireless efforts hit home in dazzling style.

Stephen couldn't hide his excitement. He grabbed his microphone and delivered a personal message to the audience: "You have no idea how much this means to me," he announced, barely audible over the roars of approval that bounced back at him from the crowd. "Thank you so, so much. This is everything I have ever wanted. It's so good to be back."

Over the next 90 minutes he was in wonderland, lapping up every round of applause and standing ovation; every banner bearing his name. Even the hard work in the gym got its first public outing as Stephen pulled off his top, pulled on a pair of green three quarter length shorts and jumped on a treadmill for a buffed-up version of *When The Going Gets Tough*. He even pulled off a half decent take on a Michael Jackson medley, grabbing his crotch and twisting his knees through a collection of the moonwalker's most famous anthems.

Stephen was jubilant as he left the stage, running straight to Louis as soon as the lights went up and hugging him tightly as he exclaimed joyously "Thank you Louis, I mean that. Thank you."

***

Over the coming nights he would settle into a familiar routine of performing, travelling and enjoying the occasional day off where he would get to reconnect with Andy.

It was around this time that Stephen called me out of the blue one Wednesday evening. He sounded in buoyant form, but wanted to get a few things off his chest. "I'd love to have a proper chat with you, you know, do a big interview or something and lay a few ghosts to rest," he said. "Can you meet me at Heathrow's Terminal 5 in the morning? I'll text you the name of the cafe when I'm there."

I could sense from Stephen that he was embracing the Boyzone comeback as a cleansing and life-changing experience. It seemed obvious to me that this interview was part of the moving on process, drawing a line under the past. I dutifully got on a plane to Heathrow the next morning and waited for him in Carluccio's Italian restaurant. Twenty minutes late, Stephen popped his head around the window. It immediately struck me how healthy he was looking – well at least from what I could see behind the dark sunglasses and tightly pulled down cap. He had a glow to his face and a genuinely contented look that I hadn't since Boyzone had split in 2000. He sat down opposite me at a table next to a gigantic window. Within seconds a group of teen fans were banging frantically on the glass to try and get his attention. Stephen flashed them a cheeky smile and a wave and they were in heaven.

We immediately got talking about his parents. "Is everything OK in that department?" I asked. Stephen was happy to set the record straight in no uncertain terms. "I would say it's still, to this day, my biggest regret. I was young and stupid and it dragged on far longer than it should have," he confessed. "I can't even remember the specifics of what started the whole thing. We certainly weren't fighting about me coming out or anything to do with my sexuality.

"We had some kind of a row or something and I was angry and I guess things got out of hand. Looking back it was a horrible time. I think I was unhappy in general and because of that it affected other parts of my life. We went a pretty long time without talking. It was crazy because you need your family and I isolated myself to a degree. In the end it was my brother Mark who called me and said, 'Look, it would be a good idea to sort this out. It's gone on too long.'"

Then Stephen told me about that trip back home: "It was so nostalgic and quite emotional. It was a lovely experience. They are still very happy there and that makes me feel so secure in a funny way. Everything changes but it stays the same, if you get my meaning."

Next Stephen's attention turned to Andy, whom he rarely spoke about in interviews. I was surprised how forthcoming he was about their private life. But Stephen seemed on a mission to spill out his every whim and emotion. He told me how they were enjoying a "perfectly normal and unremarkable" married life together in their six-bedroom home in posh Highgate, North London.

He continued: "We are best friends and we have a great marriage. I hate having anything dirty around the house so I'm always cleaning up and doing the domestic duties. Andy looks after the bills and makes sure they are all paid on time because I have a real mental block about that kind of thing."

He cringed when I asked him about the infamous photos of the pair having a punch-up outside London's trendy Ivy restaurant four years before. "We were both drunk and it was completely ridiculous," he accepted, half laughing at the whole saga in hindsight.

And the worst thing about it is Andy wasn't even attacking me any more than I was him, but because I was the one on the ground it looked like he was some kind of 6ft hefty brute giving me a kicking. He's really a softy and an extremely caring, warm person. We just have a good laugh about it now. I have to say, though, ever since that night I've never had any trouble booking a table there. They remember the publicity they got that night!

"We don't argue half as much anymore. We're much more mature about our relationship and I think you grow into each other after a while and you don't sweat the small stuff. If Andy and I have a disagreement about something we can patch it up pretty quickly. It's a nice way to be because there's not half as much negative emotions swirling around and they just bring everyone down."

I asked about his battle with depression and if he ever feared returning to that dark place: "Not really because I dealt with it properly at the time," he said, looking back on the experience with wisdom. "I think I was lucky to have the likes of Elton John coming to help me out. Without him I could have been in a really bad place. People don't see that side of Elton but I can't say enough how much he was a saviour to me. Sometimes you need someone to come and give you a good lift up and show you that life isn't all dark and doom and gloom, and he did just that."

As our time together came to an end a well-dressed Ronan Keating strolled in and pulled up a chair beside me. He was soon followed by bandmate Shane Lynch, who looked toned and muscled in a tee-shirt and jeans. I'd been following the band through their highs and lows for the past 10 years, but I couldn't recall them ever being so relaxed and at ease in each other's company.

I glanced around the table between exchanging gossip with them and wondered how rich these three Dubliners must have become as a combined force over the past decade.

I cheekily asked Stephen: "Give me the figure – have you made over £10 million?" Stephen shook his head and insisted: "I'm not telling you that, no way." "Over nine million?" I continued, willing him to give in. Finally, he conceded: "Look it's not far off if we're talking Sterling. We've all done pretty well out of Boyzone and we're well off."

With that Boyzone's tour manager Mark Plunkett reminded me that the boys had a flight to catch in 20 minutes, so despite their millions, I paid £74.50 for their lunch bill and wished them good luck on their big homecoming show. Ronan got the last word in as always: "I don't fucking believe it," he gasped, sending his bandmates into hysterics. "I've been waiting 10 years for Paul Martin to get his wallet out. It's a miracle. "And you'll be waiting another fucking 10 for the next time!" I shouted back, thanking Stephen for his time and heading for the exit.

I was left in no doubt from spending that morning with Stephen that the Boyzone comeback was far from a stage managed, begrudging reunification of five singers looking to top up their bank balances. There seemed to be a genuine camaraderie between the band – and Stephen was at its epicentre.

After Stephen performed their final concert of the tour at the Carlisle Bitts Park on 23 August 2008 his mind turned to another matter of unfinished business – reclaiming the chart dominance that had eluded him since the days of his solo career flop at the turn of the millennium.

Louis and the band had been gunning to record a version of pop star Mika's previously unreleased song, *Gave It All Away*. But the curly-haired star was far from agreeable to the concept of lending his name to a Boyzone release, and spurned their efforts.

Instead, it was settled that they would record an upbeat, if slightly underwhelming number called *Love You Anyway*.

In the video the band walked through New York streets looking sharp in designer shades and suits. Stephen, with his hair coiffured within a millimetre of its life, a large Windsor knotted tie and pocket handkerchief, looked equally as dashing as he leant on the wall on a wet sidewalk and admired a troupe of blonde dancers busting slick moves. The camera then panned to a stage managed shot of them meeting on a dark street and embracing like old friends – a message to their fans that the lost boys were back together as the dynamic force that they once had been.

For Stephen the shoot was a huge success. He had been pushing for a big budget American style jamboree that would put them in the same league as their Take That rivals when it came to big spending productions. And the end result was impressive.

Less sensational was the chart position, which peaked at number five in the UK in October 2008. It was not the number one spot they had set their hearts on, but Stephen was determined to put a brave face on it on behalf of his bandmates: "The charts have totally changed since we were last around," he said. "You have to look at the fact that we have just come off a sell-out tour and, to be honest, touring is bigger than selling records now. Ask any band or artists and it's all about the live shows rather than the charts position."

Stephen's assertion that bums on seats were more important than chart numbers would turn out to be right on the money. As 2008 ended it was concert arenas and not record sales that were firmly on Stephen's agenda. Boyzone lived by the old showbiz adage that you could never get too much of a good thing – especially when it came to bank account busting live shows.

Stephen entered the final year of his life on top of the world – with another flurry of sold out live concerts to look forward to as the band hit dizzying new heights. It was almost as if Stephen's final tour was written in the stars as he took to the stage with his Boyzone brothers in the early summer of 2009.

While the first comeback shows had been all about the

remarkable return of the pop icons, it was Stephen's name that was written all over these shows. He positively shone out a mile above his other bandmates. And fittingly, he was given his own moment in the spotlight, stirring the adoring crowd into a frenzy with his hilarious yet high paced take on Beyonce's *All The Single Ladies*.

I was lucky enough to be invited back stage to his last-ever performance in Dublin when he lapped up the hero worshipping being offered from the stalls at the o2. Stephen was in truly masterful form and even the harshest critic couldn't fault his near flawless performance, being played out in dramatic style just three streets away from his humble upbringing.He was high on energy, enthusiasm and life. He looked better than ever – his complexion radiating under the lights and a permanent grin etched on his face. He was a man who appeared to be at the peak of his health and well being. Nobody could have guessed, based on that final hurrah in his home town, of the fateful events which would unfold less than five months later. I looked around the mass of fans and it seemed every one of them was on their feet, clapping in unison as Stephen led them on a rousing chorus. It was Stephen's moment. An enduring moment for all those who were there.

That evening as Louis, *Irish Sun* showbiz writer Jennifer O'Brien and I had dinner at Marco Pierre White's steak house on Dublin's Dawson Street. Stephen called Louis around midnight and summoned us to meet him for nightcaps in the Westbury hotel. I arrived with them to find the singer and his boyfriend Andy cuddled up on a huge ornate sofa in the bar area with Shane Lynch and his wife Sheena White, sipping wine contentedly in an otherwise deserted room.

Stephen immediately leapt to his feet and greeted us each with a warm embrace, offering us drinks of our choice as he excitedly asked each of us in turn 'What did you think of the show? Did you enjoy it?" We took a straw poll and agreed Stephen had stolen the show. "That's not bad coming from two fierce tabloid journalists and an even fiercer *X Factor* judge," he joked, bursting into laughter.

Shane and Sheena made their excuses and went to bed. Stephen and Andy stayed with us for another hour talking about life, marriage, boyfriends, girlfriends and all the normal things friends chat about when they get together. Every now and again he would break into that mischievous giggle that all his friends knew so well.

"I'm really happy," he told us. "I've got the rest of the tour to look forward, to then I'm getting back to work on my book. It's going to be a really exciting year. Bring it on is what I say!"

These upbeat words of hope, optimism and excitement for the future were the last that Stephen would ever speak to me. As casually as the evening had begun, it ended. Stephen got up, wished us good night, and walked off to his room with Andy. It was the last time I ever saw him.

CHAPTER TEN
The Final Curtain

There was a chilling silence in the stark and bare waiting room as Ronan, Keith, Mikey and Shane, along with their manager Louis Walsh, prepared for the most difficult moment of their lives.

They knew not what to say. Words would have been inadequate anyway. All the years of scrapping to make it big in the music business, realising their dream in a blaze of glory and reuniting to discover their bond was stronger than ever, had all come down to this moment. A moment of unimaginable pain and anguish.

Outside, the bitterly cold evening hadn't stopped thousands of Boyzone fans, locals and mourners from every corner of the globe, congregating along the beat up streets that Stephen once called home. They held candles, banners, posters and even played Boyzone songs in a dramatic outpouring of grief, the likes of which had never been seen on the streets of Dublin before.

As the Boyzone lads stood ashen-faced and forlorn in their designer suits and polished shoes, Stephen's open casket lay in waiting through the solitary oak door of the Sheriff Street funeral home. Poignantly, the singer was dressed in a typical Boyzone sharp suit with a matching tie, a white shirt and his favourite specially made red trainers, lovingly chosen by Andrew and Stephen's mother Margaret. The trainers were a must. Custom made by Nike, they had been given to Stephen just two weeks before his death. He loved the black hand-stitching. His nickname "Steo" was inscribed into the left trainer and "Gately" to the right.

"Stephen adored them and had worn them every day since. They were a must when Andrew got to thinking about how Stephen would want to be dressed," said a family friend.

"Stephen had talked of nothing else for weeks. They were his latest fad and he'd have wanted them with him. That was Stephen all over – childlike, in the sweetest possible way."

After a private viewing at the funeral home with Stephen's Boyzone bandmates, Andrew's legs buckled beneath him. Then the moment arrived. First Andy entered the room and placed his hand gently on Stephen's, clutching a set of rosary beads. Instantly his heart melted with sorrow and despair. A friend who was told about the final farewell said: "They opened the casket just so everyone could go in to say goodbye. He looked completely peaceful, asleep and beautiful. It was hard for all concerned, a heartbreaking moment. But for Andrew who, remember, had found him and tried to save him, it was more than he could stand. His knees just gave way and he collapsed."

Stephen's bandmates entered, filing in one by one and grimacing in pain as they wrapped their arms around each other, desperately trying to summon the inner strength to confront the moment. Ronan fell against the wall as he burst into tears; Shane – a devout born again Christian – closed his eyes and turned to the power of prayer to find solace.

As they attempted to compose themselves, the boys put a red silk handkerchief in Stephen's breast pocket. It was his favourite colour and, in tribute, each band member wore something red on their own funeral suits to remember him by.

Stephen's casket was then taken to St Laurence O'Toole church where, after a short Mass for the family, the surviving members of Boyzone bunked down in the church in sleeping bags to spend the night with their beloved pal, who always hated to be alone in the dark.

His mother Margaret had asked them to make sure he was not left alone, and they obliged.

They sat beside him through the long, dark night, worried he would be lonely and scared if left all alone in an empty, echoing church. They even ordered fish and chips, and asked the parish priest if they could drink a bottle of Stephen's favourite wine to toast his final night.

They reminisced about the hundreds of great nights shared in their incredible 17 year journey. They promised he would always be with them, wherever their paths should lead. And they laughed about his nicknames for them – Kitty, Shanice, Mikeala and Rosaleen – lost in "the little bubble of humour and security" they had created for each other. Hours before the band mates had proudly displayed fresh tattoos honouring their pal. The first – "76 - 09" for the years of Stephen's birth and death – appeared beneath Superman-style S designs like the one the singer had on his chest.

They had maintained a respectful silence about their brother's passing since Ronan had addressed the world on their behalf five days before from Palma's private aircraft terminal.

During the emotional tribute he said: "Last Saturday our world changed forever when we lost our friend and brother Stephen. We have come to Majorca today to accompany our pal on his final journey back to Dublin, where we know he will be given an unforgettable send off tomorrow. We'd like to thank the authorities here for their help and for the respect they have shown to our friend."

Ronan's voice began to falter as he said: "The countless messages of love and support we have received this week have truly overwhelmed ourselves and the Gately family. We thank you from the bottom of our hearts for each and every one of them. We would also like to thank the media for respecting our privacy this week and ask that you continue to do so tomorrow."

Ronan tried to keep his head high but changes in his voice prompted a tightening of Mikey Graham's supportive arm around him as he said: "Stephen lived to perform and truly loved being centre stage. You can be sure he's looking down on us, wishing we'd move over so he could flash his smile for the cameras one more time."

Back in the church, just before daylight filtered through the stained-glass window of St Laurence O'Toole church, the lads ended their 10-hour vigil, whispering their tearful farewells before the rest of Dublin gathered to say goodbye. The boys thanked fans who had queued all night outside the church to get a good view of the funeral. They donated their sleeping bags to three English fans that were among the crowd who camped out all night.

Sue Morris, a 56 year old fan, said: "The boys came over and thanked us for coming. Then moments later one of their managers handed us three sleeping bags, telling us the boys wanted us to have them because it was so cold out here." The prison worker from Nottingham added: "I brought along a black trilby hat I managed to catch when Stephen threw it from the stage at a gig. I've been a Boyzone fan for 17 years and even have a tattoo where Shane signed my arm. They looked devastated and I told them we knew what they were going through. Shane said it was hard in there but they wouldn't have missed it for the world. We told them we'll keep supporting them if they go on without Stephen, but would understand if it was too hard for them. I think they will carry on to keep his memory alive."

Floral tributes left on the church railings included a white teddy bear carrying a rose with the message: "Stephen, you are an angel in the sky. You reached everyone through your smile, a heart and voice of gold. Please look after Ronan, Keith, Shane and Mikey from above."

By the time the church bell began tolling solemnly at 11.40 a.m., people were crowded on balconies, clinging to lamp posts and hanging precariously out of windows to get a better view. The local hair salon started selling tea and coffee to thirsty fans. Residents close to the church sold window space to photographers and one local lass sold white roses to throw at the coffin.

Alan Hunter, a former local radio DJ, laughed: "Stephen would think it's great they're making a few bob out of him. It's the Dublin spirit. Everyone loved him."

Outside thousands of fans who had camped overnight shared the pavements with journalists, Sky News camera crews, satellite trucks and Garda officers. As each member of the "Boyzone family" arrived, they were greeted by cheers, the likes of which would have seemed more suited to a pop concert than a sombre funeral.

Louis Walsh emerged from a car with his close friend Caroline Desmond, wife of MCD concert promoter Dennis. He removed his glasses and walked cross to the waiting camera crews to pay tribute to his tragic protégé, as well as to the loyalty and love shown by his band mates.

"They were his best mates, they were his family, they were the best friends in the world," Louis explained as reporters and cameramen hung on his every word. "And they knew the real Stephen, the Stephen who never offended anyone in his life."

Celebrities arrived in their droves, from pop stars like Westlife, Jason O'Donovan and Brian McFadden, to TV personalities including Vanessa Feltz. Stephen's parents and friends arrived at the church with Andrew, and then the Boyzone lads emerged, and were greeted with cheers and applause. Inside there were four pictures of Stephen near the altar, along with his favourite photo of the band. Each pew was adorned with white roses, lilies and hydrangeas. Their scent filled the air as stars and politicians took their seats for the requiem mass.

It was a celebration of his life, a service of laughter and tears – one the lads knew Stephen would approve of. Parish Priest Father Declan Blake spoke of "the terrible darkness that descended when we heard the shocking news of Stephen's death". He added: "We thank God for Stephen's life."

Boyzone made their way to the altar to perform their tribute to Stephen. They gave a heart-rending performance of Westlife's hit *In This Life*, with its poignant line: "*If it all falls apart, I will know deep in my heart, the only dream that mattered had come true, in this life I was loved by you.*"

Stephen's quirky sense of humour was evident too in the gifts carefully chosen by friends and family and left with the coffin as part of the offertory procession during the funeral mass. They included a pair of Mickey Mouse ears, because he had a lifelong love of everything Disney, and a tub of his favourite La Prairie moisturiser, which he insisted on using twice a day. Shortly before his death, he had told a friend: "I should buy shares in La Prairie; I can't get enough of it." Also included was a top hat, in recognition of his love for performing and showmanship which had led him – following the Boyzone split – to go on to the West End stage where he was building an acclaimed career after appearing in several musicals. There was a bouquet of white lilies laid on the coffin too and – as a memento of his 2006 civil partnership with internet entrepreneur Andrew – a copy of their wedding breakfast menu.

The band members gathered at the lectern to read a eulogy. Keith called Stephen "a true performer, full of life and spirit". Mikey drew gales of laughter as he recalled how pint-sized Stephen asked

Louis Walsh at their early auditions: "How tall do ya have to be to be in Boyzone?" Mikey added: "He was a giant of a man in our hearts." Ronan told how Stephen loved to laugh and make up dirty jokes. But his voice broke as spoke of "a beautiful man, a friend, a brother, a son, a husband and a hero".

Then the grieving stars performed their final task for Stephen. Along with his brother Tony and tour manager Mark Plunkett, they gently lifted his casket on their shoulders and carried it out into the sunlight. The wave of love that greeted Stephen brought fresh tears to their eyes.

Stephen's passion for performing had taken him from the tough Northside neighbourhood to the pinnacle of pop success, and as Louis Walsh had predicted, Dublin gave their local hero an unforgettable send-off.

Deborah Monaghan, 31, used to play with Stephen when they were at primary school together and had brought her seven year old daughter, Lauren, to say goodbye. She said: "It's like one great big family funeral. Stephen was one of us and will always be one of us. Even when he hit the big time, he never forgot his roots. He always came home to his family, looked after his friends and if he passed you in the street, stopped for a chat. He inspired other kids to follow their dream. And that's really something when you grow up in a tough area."

For Stephen's mentor, father figure and friend Louis Walsh, the loss was unbearable. "I was completely broken," he revealed. "I just can't get my head around it and don't know how I'll get over it. I've just been walking around in a daze. I am still in shock. I just cannot believe this has happened. I have lost my best friend."

Louis says that Stephen was one of the nicest people he'd ever met – as well as being a huge heartthrob who always had time for his fans. "He was just amazingly fun, honest, relaxing, and so good natured," he said. "You have no idea. We were always having a laugh, always. When I had screaming girls outside he was the only one that would still come out and sign autographs, even at the end. He didn't change. They all changed a bit, but Stephen never changed. He would do anything for his fans."

He recalled how Stephen was great fun, as well as being a huge fan of *The X Factor*. "He used to text me during *X Factor*, telling me who he liked and who he didn't," he says. "He'd always send me funny texts. He was like a child. He loved Celine Dion and Mariah. And he lived for Disney. We had some incredible nights in London. We'd go to the Ivy, always somewhere fabulous. We'd get drunk, gossip, have fun, fall around being silly.

"He came from Sheriff Street. He was a very working class kid. All he wanted to do was sing and go to the West End. Of all the people I've worked with, I don't think anybody thanked me as much as Stephen. He'd always say to me, 'If I wasn't in Boyzone I don't know where I'd be today; thank you. A great, great, professional kid.'"

Louis went on to recall how Stephen took the break-up of Boyzone in 2000 after a succession of hit records. He said: "All Stephen lived for was to be singing music. He was down because the band was his life and they were his best friends, and it was finished. But he picked himself up and got on to the West End. I think he was the glue in the band because he kept everybody happy."

As time passes and the healing begins, the singer's bandmates are bravely facing a future without their brightest star. Ronan confessed how they struggled to cope in the shocking aftermath of his passing. "It was horrible, you can't breathe, you feel like your chest is collapsing, the walls are coming in on top of you. Anxiety I think is what they call it. It's been horrible. We've all been feeling the same way since Stephen passed. Mentally I'm absolutely exhausted. I've never before thought about going to get help with counsellors. For the first time ever I think I should. When I lost my mum it was the hardest thing at the time that I'd ever known in my life, but because she was sick for two years and we were told three months before she died that she had three months left, subconsciously you build a wall, your defence mechanism goes up and you prepare yourself for that. Whereas with Steo, there was nothing, just this wall of devastation, shock. I don't think it has hit any of us properly. There's times when you feel like you can't breathe, you know, when you're panicking and I'm not like that. I've always been on a level."

The front man recalled finding out the terrible news about Stephen: "I bawled my eyes out. Screamed down the phone: 'What are you saying?' I couldn't take it in. When the guy on the phone said 'Stephen passed away' I said 'Stephen who?' because I thought he was talking about someone else. I just didn't think it would be Steo. I'll never forget it. I ran out of the restaurant, and my sister ran after me with my coat saying 'What's wrong, what's wrong?' I told her. And then I had to call the three guys. Bloody hell, what a call.

Horrendous. The most horrendous hour of my life. Horrific."

Keith was equally as distraught. He confessed: "I have waves of emotion that can hit me at any time. In the first few weeks they were terrifying. I couldn't breathe. I'd go light-headed and it was incredibly frightening. They still come, but I can handle them better now. I was distraught. I felt anger; disbelief. I cried a lot and had terrible nightmares. But I believe Stephen's in a better place now, he's looking over us and he's happy.

"Stephen brought out our nurturing sides – we'd think nothing of hugging and kissing each other. And he got us into pampering! We were into our flash cars, but Stephen would just spend thousands on beauty products. He got us into expensive face creams – we were the gayest straight band in the world and we loved him for it.

"It was a massive loss and there are times when I still can't believe it happened. Stephen was the glue between us in Boyzone and when he passed, a lot of my confidence went. But apart from how sad I feel, I feel sorry for Stephen. He was so young and had his whole life ahead of him, and he was absolutely robbed.

"The day after he passed was so surreal. Usually when we're all at the airport together, we get people coming up to us, but there were TV screens all around the airport. It was all over the news and nobody said a word to us because everyone knew what had happened. Mikey got some Irish breakfasts and Shane got six bottles of beer, and nobody would charge us for anything. We were doing our best to keep it together, but when that happened, we were in bits with tears streaming down our faces."

The last word should remain with Andy, his devoted husband and best friend – the man with whom Stephen could finally be himself. Understandably, the grief is still raw. He packed a suitcase, left the house that he and Stephen shared, and hasn't been back since. "I never needed belongings, but Stephen was very house-proud, so everything in there is what he chose, and there are too many ghosts," he said.

Their two dogs – Bentley and Charlie – have been adopted by friends and Andrew is grateful for the distraction of his business. "You don't have the luxury of falling to pieces when you have customers and staff to manage." He has been back to their holiday home in Majorca a couple of times. To his relief, "There was no bad vibe, because Stephen was happy there, and so was I." One of his greatest comforts, he says, "is knowing that Stephen was a happy man. He had gone from being lost and insecure to really knowing who he was. It was like arriving at a destination – he'd got to where he wanted to be in life. I just can't help feeling cheated that he didn't get to stay at that destination for longer."

***

Such pain will be eased through the passages of time. And his band mates are already preparing to pay the ultimate, joyous tribute to Stephen by taking to the stage – possibly one last time – to tour in his memory. Whether it's the singer's closest bandmates, his beloved manager, his adoring family or his loyal fans, everyone agrees that Stephen Gately lived the dream. He wasn't the first street urchin to imagine himself receiving the adulation of millions on the football field, or in the boxing ring, or on the silver screen, or standing in the spotlight on the stage of one of the world's great arenas, and he certainly won't be the last.

For the spindly, confused little kid from Sherriff Street, the dream became a reality because he had the talent, the drive, the ambition and the charisma to make it happen when the chance to win fame and fortune tapped him on the shoulder. Were he to audition for X Factor today, the contest would in all probability be over virtually before it started, because people like Louis Walsh and Simon Cowell know star quality the moment they see it, and Stephen had star quality in abundance.

Google his name today and close to 400,000 results will appear on your screen, almost as many as are available for the entire Boyzone band. His untimely death, and some of the controversy which surrounded it, undoubtedly has something to do with this enduring popularity, but there is also no doubt that as a performer he was admired and adored as one of the leading pop artists of his time, albeit a time cut all too short in the most tragic and unpredictable of circumstances.

There are still tens of thousands of young people who cherish his memory, even though many aspects of his showbiz career are chequered, and open to a more cynical interpretation. Would he have made it to the top had not Louis Walsh seen his boyish charm and cheeky manner as a central component of a manufactured band, that would, first and foremost, be the right thing at the right time, even if its total was far greater than the sum of its individual parts? Did Stephen have what it takes to carve out a career for himself without the help of a pop Svengali who knew every trick in the book? It doesn't really matter.

The world of celebrity is liberally sprinkled with stories of stars whose light would have shone unnoticed but for a chance encounter, a simple twist of fate, or a single defining moment which enabled them to emerge from the obscurity of their personal dream world. Would he have ever plucked up the courage to acknowledge and celebrate his own sexuality had not an opportunistic employee sold him out to the tabloid newspaper with the most cash to splash?

We will never know, but we do know that before his death at 33, Stephen was a member of a band that recorded six UK number one hits and five number one albums, and sold more than 20 million records around the world. That fact alone earns him his place in music legend.

That he then rose so magnificently to the challenge of playing the leading role in an Andrew Lloyd Webber musical on the West End Stage, and was on the verge of publishing his first novel, seems to confirm that the mean streets of Dublin were never going to hold on to the baby-faced boy with the holes in his jumper and the cardboard in his shoes.

Picture Credits

Plate Section 1

Pages 1, 4, 5, 6, 7 top, 7 bottom, 8 top, 9, 10, 11, 12 bottom, 13, 14 top, 14 bottom, 15, 16 © Irish Daily Mirror

Pages 2, 3 top, 3 bottom, 8 bottom, 12 top © Collins Picture Agency Dublin

Plate Section 2

Pages 1, 3, 4, 8, 9, 10, 11, 16 bottom © Irish Daily Mirror

Pages 2, 5, 6, 12, 13, 14, 15, 16 top © Collins Picture Agency Dublin

Page 7 © Brian McEvoy Photography